Praise for *Swipe Right*

"I believe with my whole heart that *Swipe Right* is going to inspire and challenge you, and not only that, but could redirect the course of your life and relationships. You might not be in a relationship, or maybe you've had many, but no matter who you are, my husband wrote this book for you. The truth, hope, and humor that drip from these pages are incredible. It's a book that needed to be written, my husband poured his heart into it, and I'm excited for all that God has for you as you read it. Buckle up."

—Jennie Lusko

"My friend Levi is an expert at prese   way. In *Swipe Right* he provides a refr   challenges our culture is facing concer..... .... spective I believe we need now more than ever."

—Steven Furtick
Pastor, Elevation Church, and *New York Times* bestselling author

"One day, someday, there will be a day when you will need the down-to-earth wisdom in this book like you need oxygen. Because as Levi so aptly appropriates, our approach to sex and romance is of life-and-death importance—at least if you care at all about your soul, that hidden thing at the core of who we are that filters the way we experience everything we do in life and death, for better or for worse. And at the core of this book is a soul-watering desire to see yours be better, in a world that increasingly seems to be settling for worse. Levi makes the taboo seem candid; the old-school, the new-school; and the difficult, more than just possible but altogether lifesaving."

—Joel Houston
Songwriter, Hillsong United, and pastor, Hillsong NYC

"I love that Levi is bringing to light the life-and-death power of sex and romance for such a time as this. I have two daughters, and there is a new level of crazy lately in the world. You should thank God that this book is in your hands. *Swipe Right* is a timely, wonderful, prophetic, and needed message for our generation."

—Christine Caine
Founder of the A21 Campaign and bestselling author of *Unashamed*

"Helpful. Timely. Needed. *Swipe Right* does what few dating books can: it calls us to a life of purity, fidelity, and honor, not in hopes of earning the perfect mate, but because we already have the hope of heaven and perfection of Jesus in our hearts. I am so grateful God has raised up Levi Lusko to be a voice of truth and grace-covered conviction for this generation. If you are wondering what God's plans are for your love life, or leading those in search of his plan for theirs, you need this book."

> —Louie Giglio
> Pastor of Passion City Church, founder of Passion
> Conferences, and author of *The Comeback*

"Sex is wonderful. Sex is powerful. According to Levi, while sex is the source of great pleasure, it has the potential to cause great pain. *In Swipe Right* Levi leverages his past as well as principles from the New Testament to help readers make better decisions and live with fewer regrets."

> —Andy Stanley
> Pastor, North Point Community Church, and author of *Deep and Wide: Creating Churches Unchurched People Love to Attend*

"When it comes to sex, dating, and marriage, most of us would agree things aren't going well. We want something different, something better. Levi Lusko has written a game-changing book on pursuing the relationship God truly wants you to have. His book *Swipe Right: The Life-and-Death Power of Sex and Romance* is funny and engaging, while simultaneously practical and hard-hitting. It's full of in-your-face truth that will empower you to love your future spouse in a healthy and God-honoring way."

> —Craig Groeschel
> Pastor of Life.Church and author of *From This Day Forward: Five Commitments to Fail-Proof Your Marriage*

"I wish this book had been around in 1970. I wish someone had handed it to a fifteen-year-old kid in West Texas. I wish someone had said to him, 'Lucado, quit listening to the locker-room lectures on sex. Listen to what God says.' The book wasn't around back then, but it is here today. And Levi Lusko has a good word, not just for fifteen-year-old boys but for all of us to suffer the consequences of a sex-saturated society. This is a good book. Study it, ponder it, and if you know a fifteen-year-old, tell them to read it."

> —Max Lucado
> *New York Times* bestselling author

"I was raised in the home of a woman who married and divorced five times. I have seen firsthand the sadness and loneliness that come as a result of turning from God's plans for relationships. God has his hand on Levi Lusko, and I believe that the word of God that Levi points to in *Swipe Right* is a much-needed drink of water in a desert of heartache."

—Greg Laurie
Pastor, Harvest Christian Fellowship, and author of
Tell Someone: You Can Share the Good News

"Thank God for people like Levi Lusko who are dedicated to bringing light to the issues that we all face. *Swipe Right* is an inspirational look at love, sex, and romance and highlights what our generation so often misses. I believe this resource will help many to understand the true power and true beauty God intends for us in these important areas of life."

—Ben Houston
Pastor, Hillsong LA

"The world begs us to view sex and romance through the distorted lens it has created. But Levi boldly approaches these topics with truth, honesty, wit, and biblical wisdom to point us back to God's original plan for us. I really believe we need the *Swipe Right* message now more than ever before."

—Lysa TerKeurst
New York Times bestselling author and
president of Proverbs 31 Ministries

"Levi Lusko is in touch with a generation searching for truth and moral clarity. In *Swipe Right* he makes the case for sexual purity in a way that connects the culture with God's principles for relationships. Every page is written with authenticity and saturated with grace and power. If you want to live a fulfilling life without regrets and experience a future with promise, this book is for you."

—Dr. Jack Graham
Pastor, Prestonwood Baptist Church, and author of *Angels:
Who They Are, What They Do, and Why It Matters*

"In a cultural climate that attempts to treat the sacred nature of relationship and sexual intimacy as casual, Levi Lusko has yielded his pen to God's hand to share what is paramount on God's heart. *Swipe Right* is the clarion call this generation needs in order to understand that God is not keeping you from a thing; he's keeping you *for* a thing. The lie of the enemy is that we can easily recover from premature sexual intimacy without incident. A loving God knows otherwise. With love, balance, wit, and humor, Levi has crafted a book that will inform generations to come. This book isn't about ceasing external behaviors that don't honor God. It's about living for God and loving God in a way where we honor his word—even regarding sex—when it is not convenient. And we do so because we love him!"

—John Gray
Associate teaching pastor, Lakewood Church,
and author of *I Am Number 8*

"Thank you, Levi, for speaking so plainly and powerfully to what is wreaking havoc among so many today. To say that *Swipe Right* is an important book for all of us would be quite an understatement. We all relate to the pages of this book. This is a word for right now, a warning sign for the days and culture we are now living. I appreciate the direct and honest way Levi approaches the power of temptation, lust, romance, and love. As I read this book, I kept hearing the words of Jesus: 'The thief comes to steal, kill, and destroy . . . but I have come that you might have life to the full.' May this book spur you on to a full, abundant life instead of one that is empty and stolen. This is more than just a book; it's a life jacket!"

—Chris Tomlin
Grammy Award–winning musician and author of *Good Good Father*

"I believe that if you want to know God's way, you must learn to follow people who know and live God's Word. Levi has faithfully walked on this journey, wherever God has led him. Through amazing triumphs and devastating valleys. Relationship navigation doesn't have to be the scavenger hunt so many people make it. Levi shows that God will light our way, if we allow him to."

—Carl Lentz
Pastor, Hillsong NYC

"In a time of relationships riddled with confusion and rattled by unnecessary heartbreak, I'm excited that Levi is sharing his scripturally founded wisdom with us. It's my hope that whoever reads this will have their thoughts of the heart as seriously provoked as mine have been. Beyond Levi's knowledge on the issues of relationships, his true heart for people is what drives him to help point us at not just the real and clear problems but the purely focused solution."

—Ryan Good
Producer, writer, and entrepreneur

SWIPE RIGHT

SWIPE RIGHT

THE LIFE-AND-DEATH POWER

OF SEX AND ROMANCE

LEVI LUSKO

W PUBLISHING GROUP

AN IMPRINT OF THOMAS NELSON

Published in Nashville, Tennessee, by W Publishing, an imprint of Thomas Nelson.

Published in association with the literary agency of Woglemuth & Associates, Inc.

Thomas Nelson titles may be purchased in bulk for educational, business, fund-raising, or sales promotional use. For information, please e-mail SpecialMarkets@ThomasNelson.com.

Any Internet addresses, phone numbers, or company or product information printed in this book are offered as a resource and are not intended in any way to be or to imply an endorsement by Thomas Nelson, nor does Thomas Nelson vouch for the existence, content, or services of these sites, phone numbers, companies, or products beyond the life of this book.

Unless otherwise noted, Scripture quotations are taken from the New King James Version®. © 1982 by Thomas Nelson. Used by permission. All rights reserved.

Scripture quotations marked THE MESSAGE are from *The Message*. Copyright © by Eugene H. Peterson 1993, 1994, 1995, 1996, 2000, 2001, 2002. Used by permission of NavPress. All rights reserved. Represented by Tyndale House Publishers, Inc.

Scripture quotations marked NIV are from the Holy Bible, New International Version®, NIV®. Copyright © 1973, 1978, 1984, 2011 by Biblica, Inc.® Used by permission of Zondervan. All rights reserved worldwide. www.zondervan.com. The "NIV" and "New International Version" are trademarks registered in the United States Patent and Trademark Office by Biblica, Inc.®

Scripture quotations marked NLT are from the Holy Bible, New Living Translation. © 1996, 2004, 2007, 2013, 2015 by Tyndale House Foundation. Used by permission of Tyndale House Publishers, Inc., Carol Stream, Illinois 60188. All rights reserved.

Scripture quotations marked PHILLIPS are from The New Testament in Modern English by J. B. Phillips. Copyright © 1960, 1972 J. B. Phillips. Administered by the Archbishops' Council of the Church of England. Used by permission.

ISBN 978-0-7180-3215-9 (SC)
ISBN 978-0-7180-3583-9 (eBook)

Library of Congress Cataloging-in-Publication Data
Library of Congress Control Number: 2016917499

Printed in the United States of America

17 18 19 20 21 LSC 10 9 8 7 6 5 4 3 2 1

*To my Jenniflower: Thank you for waiting
for me and giving me your key. You have
ravished my heart. I will love you all my days.*

Contents

Contents

Chapter Zero

I just broke my neck.
  I was lying on my back in the snow, wearing a full-face motorcycle helmet. I could hear the snowmobile idling next to me. It sat upright and intact, waiting for me to hop back on, squeeze the throttle, and join my friends doing figure eights in the powdery wonderland that is Montana in the winter. But I couldn't jump up, and I would never ride a snowmobile again. My neck was broken.

The snap of the bone had sounded like a muffled gunshot in my ears. I remember seeing the ditch beyond the berm at the last second, followed by a vague sinking feeling as I processed that I was going much too fast to stop. I had felt myself rising out of the saddle the way you would if gravity were turned off, bringing me to a standing position in the air; and then, as though a dream were ending, the ground had come toward me much too quickly. The snowmobile met the earth on the front skis, and my body crumpled against the handlebars just before it was discarded onto the snow.

I quickly tried to move my arms and turn my head and was relieved to find I could do both. As I continued my systems check and scanned the rest of my body, an alarm sounded in my brain. My left leg was pointing away from my body at a forty-five-degree angle, bent at a hinge halfway between my knee and my hip that had never existed before. Seeing it lie there so inappropriately, I somehow fought off panic. *I can fix this. I just need to get that leg straightened out,* I thought.

I willed my legs to move, and the right one responded as normal. The left one was a different story. From the new joint down, there was no movement at all. When I tried harder, I found a section of bone, about the length of a pirate's wooden peg leg, connected to my hip to be the only part paying attention. The rest of my leg was just a nonresponsive sack of Jell-O lying sideways in the snow while this tiny peg leg moved freely inside my thigh. It was then, with sickening clarity, I realized the sound of bone breaking had come from inside my leg. For some reason I worried about being able to climb the stairs to the stage at church next Sunday.

Those worries were short lived, as waves of nausea surged through my body. Suddenly I felt claustrophobic. I needed to get my helmet off.

I waved my arms in the air, trying desperately to signal my friends, who had been doing their absolute best to destroy all the pristine powder in sight on their own snowmobiles. It took some time to get their attention, but they eventually saw I had been ejected and was lying on the ground. They took one look at me and called 911.

We were in the middle of nowhere, thirty miles from the

Canadian border. When the ambulance eventually arrived, volunteer paramedics carried me on a stretcher through waist-deep snow before loading me up for the bumpy ride.

"Can you give him some drugs?" my friend Greg asked a paramedic in response to my moaning every time we hit a pothole.

"Unfortunately, as volunteers, we aren't authorized to provide medication," the paramedic replied.

When we reached the city limits, another ambulance was waiting on the side of the road, and I was transferred into a vehicle full of people who were allowed to give me morphine. This is where my memory gets hazy, but Greg tells me I got really chatty and spent the rest of the ride inviting the paramedics to come to church with me sometime. Clearly I was no longer intimidated by the stairs.

The good news was that I had cleared the ditch. The bad news was that when I had landed in a standing position against the handlebars, my femur had snapped in half.

"Congratulations," the ER doc told me. "You managed to break the biggest bone in your body."

I have only flashes of recollection from the next couple of days. I hazily remember my wife and two daughters being at the hospital, and I recall being angry when I realized my favorite pair of jeans had been cut off of me. At some point my dad leaned over my hospital bed, looking concerned.

I spent the night in traction until a surgeon was available to turn me into Wolverine, putting eighteen inches of titanium into the two pieces of my femur and securing it with pins at the top and bottom.

As in almost all difficult circumstances, in the aftermath

there were blessings to count and reasons to be thankful. One of my doctors told me of someone who had broken a leg in the same way but had severed the femoral artery in the process and had bled out in the snow before help could arrive.

For the record, I am thankful. I am also woozy and have gotten light-headed several times as I relived this memory to share it with you.

YOU'VE GOT THE POWER

But this is not a book about broken bones or snowmobiles. It is a book about power and the way powerful things can be used to do great good or great damage. Channeled properly, the same forces that can destroy you can propel you to places you never could get to otherwise. It's all in the application of strength.

My physical therapist told me that the femur breaks he has treated are usually caused by either car and motorcycle accidents or football injuries. Broken bones require a collision. Power.

The snowmobile is an amazing invention. Humanity has figured out how to pack the power of five hundred horses into a vehicle so that moving from one place to

> Channeled properly, the same forces that can destroy you can propel you to places you never could get to otherwise.

another is faster. Such an engine that propels a sled and its rider over snow would have dropped jaws one thousand years ago. In days gone by, dogsleds were the only option to get medicine to Nome, Alaska, but no longer. I imagine the snowmobile has saved many lives—but I can tell you from experience that it also has the power to break a bone as though it were balsa wood.

We are living in extraordinary times. More has changed on this planet since the Industrial Revolution (the 1700s to 1900s) than in all the preceding years of recorded history. And the exponential change in the last thirty years is mind-boggling. In my short lifetime, the Internet was developed, has become widely available, and can now be accessed by the cell phones of billions of people. That's a lot of power in a small device I can easily put in my back pocket.

I know of nothing more powerful on earth than the forces of love, sex, and romance. The potential for pleasure, joy, strength, and blessing is virtually immeasurable. With that great power comes the opportunity for not just beauty and blessing, but also great danger. It's like a Tesla in Ludicrous Mode that can go zero to sixty in under three seconds: it can feel amazing taking off but also has enough power to get you into trouble. Solomon, the wisest man who ever lived, said that you can't build a fire in your lap and not burn your pants (Proverbs 6:27 THE MESSAGE).

> You can't build a fire in your lap and not burn your pants.

SCREEN TIME

For better or worse, interactions with screens are now irreversibly enmeshed into the fabric of our lives. We swipe right to answer calls, unlock our phones, respond to snaps, browse through photos, and reply to e-mails. With our fingertips dancing across devices, we navigate our lives. It is now estimated that the average American pulls his or her phone out to check it one hundred and fifty times each day. That's once every six minutes.[1]

As a millennial, loosely defined as those born between 1982 and 2002, I am part of a transitional generation. I grew up knowing how to use a typewriter, I licked stamps, I rented movies at Blockbuster on Friday nights (and had to rewind them before returning them to avoid a fee), and I looked up information for projects in the *Encyclopædia Britannica*. I called in to request songs I wanted to hear on the radio and made bootleg copies when they played on my boom box so I could listen to them on my Walkman. How violently things have been transformed. My daughters will never know life without Siri, Amazon Prime, and Wikipedia. They don't know the struggle of respooling a cassette tape with a pencil. They will never understand the pterodactyl-like sounds that emitted from a modem before the dial-up connection signed on to AOL. They won't recall what it was like not to be able to end arguments on Google while binge-watching a series on Netflix (not the Netflix that came in the mail one disc at a time but the one that is available at all hours on every screen in your life).

In so many ways the world is better because of all the

tech upgrades, but with this great power has come the ability to break a man's bones and "by means of a harlot" reduce his life "to a crust of bread" (Proverbs 6:26). The Internet has brought porn and apps that make a casual sexual encounter as easy as swiping to the right. Dating apps such as OkCupid, Grindr, and Tinder have poured gasoline onto what was already a hookup culture.

Tinder alone has more than a *trillion* swipes now. You swipe to the left if you are not interested in the person or to the right if you are, and if you both choose each other, you can begin to communicate. It is no doubt that apart from the swiping function Tinder never would have become the behemoth it is, but "swiping right" has become so much bigger than the app that pioneered it. In an article in *Wired* magazine, David Pierce wrote, "In the . . . years since Tinder's launch, the right swipe has become the prevailing signifier of our generation—shorthand for like, lust, and (possibly, hopefully, finally) love."[2]

It is impossible to overstate what a gamechanger this all is.

Justin Garcia, a research scientist at Indiana University's Kinsey Institute for Research in Sex, Gender, and Reproduction, noted that in the last four million years, two key transitions have changed how men and women mate: "The first was . . . in the agricultural revolution. . . . And the second major transition is with the rise of the Internet."[3]

There are now more than one hundred million people on mobile dating apps; half of those are on Tinder.[4] No-strings-attached sexual encounters are becoming increasingly convenient to arrange as fast as you can swipe across your screen. At the same time, fewer and fewer of the users of these apps are interested in marriage—or any kind of commitment—as the context for sexual experiences, because it is so easy to, in the words of one mobile dater, "hit it and quit it."[5]

My generation and those following have stripped sex of any emotional or spiritual significance, and now it is simply viewed as a physical source of pleasure and enjoyment. A twenty-nine-year-old quoted in a shockingly honest article in *Rolling Stone* titled "Tales From the Millennials' Sexual Revolution" claimed point-blank that sex is "a piece of body touching another piece of body—just as existentially meaningless as kissing."[6] My question is this: At what cost? The laws of the universe dictate that there are equal and opposite reactions for every action—or, to get biblical, we reap what we sow. Just what exactly is all this porn and recreational sex doing to us on the inside?

The paint is still wet. It is impossible to know what the additions of text messaging, Instagram, Snapchat, and Pokémon have done to our lives, attention spans, and intelligence. God knows they haven't helped us to become better drivers or conversationalists. Emoji have become a way of life. *Pizza is bae. Winky face. Laughing until I am crying.*

I am not suggesting you delete your social media accounts, buy a butter churn, or try to find a Blockbuster video store. I am eagerly awaiting the delivery of packages by drones, Uber beats a taxi all day long, and I don't know what I would do without Waze. What I *am* suggesting is that when it comes to love, sex, and romance, perhaps the best approach is not new-and-improved but old-school. And don't get me wrong: it's not connecting with people over the

Internet or the swiping of screens that is the problem. We just need to swipe right—to live *up* in a left/right world.

I'M SORRY, YOU'RE BREAKING UP

Integrity, purity, fidelity, monogamy. Although these words might sound as if they belong in a museum, I believe they are God's plans for our relationships—plans that are not only the paths to our greatest pleasures but the keys to our greatest power. And believe me, God wants to use you powerfully. He is all about you enjoying the awesome gift that is sex—that's why he thought of it. He's not holding out on you. It's actually quite the opposite: he has much he wants to give you. Unfortunately when you take a bite from what God has told you not to eat, it can keep you from experiencing what he wants you to have (Genesis 2:17). Father knows best.

Are you still with me? Or are you thinking I'm going to squeeze your finger into Joe Jonas's purity ring? Are you worried I'll suggest you buy your daily latte only at HeBrews coffee shop, watch videos only at GodTube, and reject all friend invitations unless they came from Faithbook? (Insert Ned Flanders-y laughter.) You might be ready to chuck this book across the room now that I've tipped my hand and shown you that, in an ever-evolving world, I'm peddling what you likely consider to be outdated, outmoded, and irrelevant relationship advice.

If you feel that way, then nothing I am going to say here will change your mind. I won't try to argue that women experience far fewer orgasms in non-committed sexual encounters[7] or lecture you about the invisible emotional scars caused by abortions.[8] No data I give you on third marriages doing worse than second marriages, or second marriages failing more than first marriages,[9] is going to dissuade you if you have already decided that times are a-changing and you are changing with them.

Just do me a favor: don't throw this book in the trash after you close it. Banish it from your thoughts if you must, but keep it. Stick it in that shoebox on the top shelf of your closet or under the socks in your dresser, and then proceed with the disposable relationships that are rampant in our culture. Feel free to spend as many years as you need in the spin cycle of hooking up, shacking up, and breaking up . . . and repeat as necessary. Do whatever you feel like doing. I just want this book tucked away somewhere safe, so that if you ever come to a place of sadness and regret, if there is ever a desperate emptiness over what porn and casual sex have brought into your heart, if you ever feel somewhat numb and broken on the inside—it'll be there waiting for you. I will be there too. Not to rub your nose in your mistakes, but to have a chat about a different strategy for harnessing the powerful gift that is sex—and then about where exactly it is you should go from there.

(If it *is* now fifteen years in the future, and your heart *has* been busted into smithereens, and you've *just now* dug this dusty copy out of a shoebox, might I suggest you jump straight to chapter 8 to read about Samson's hair growing back? You'll find some good news there before doubling back to the beginning. Just please tell me there are finally *real* hoverboards like the ones in *Back to the Future II*, because the things that went by that name while I was writing this book did not deserve to use the word. *Winky face.*)

The day I broke my leg was the first time I set foot in that particular emergency room, but it wouldn't be my last. Five years later I would find myself there once more. Again it was winter, and I was with my wife, Jennie, and our daughter Lenya on the night Lenya unexpectedly went to heaven. I wrote my first book, *Through the Eyes of a Lion*, about that experience, because no matter who you are or where you live, you will go through tragedy and loss. I felt burdened to help prepare people for trials they are not yet in, to see the power that exists in the midst of pain.

I am writing this book, *Swipe Right*, to help you train for the relationship you are not yet in, and to help you see God's plans for it. I write because of the power you have right now to bring about a future that thrills you or one that crushes bones and reduces your life to a crust of bread. I write as a father of four daughters, to share with you the same basic stuff that my wife and I spent last night discussing with our oldest daughter. Over a candlelight dinner at a fancy restaurant, we did a lot of listening and talked with her about sex, romance, marriage, choices, and the power of the present to impact the future. You might be old enough to be my mom, but maybe no one has ever told you how valuable and special you are, and that you don't need to pimp your body for the worth you crave but already have and can never lose. Ultimately I write so you can never ask, with sadness and regret, "If you knew I was heading full speed toward a ditch, why didn't you say something?" Sex and romance are not peripheral to your life; they are of life-and-death importance.

I'm going to level with you here: I'm no expert. I don't have this all figured out. I want to ask questions, not just give answers.

My goal is for you to make progress, not to achieve perfection. That would just set you up for disappointment when you fall short.

> My goal is for you to make progress, not to achieve perfection.

I haven't lived out everything I think you should do.

I need to read the truth in this book as much as I need to write it. I echo what C. S. Lewis said: looking inside myself I find "a zoo of lusts, a bedlam of ambitions . . . a harem of fondled hatreds."[10] Divorce goes back as far as I can search in my family tree on both sides, and I desperately want that to end with me. I am not immune to the temptations I am bombarded by, and if I compromise and put myself in the wrong place, I could do in minutes what I would regret for decades.

The truth is that I'm a hot mess, but I believe what I am going to tell you with all my heart, and I feel strongly enough about it that I think it would be sin for me not to write this book.

This won't all be easy to read; these are complex, emotionally charged issues we are going to talk about. There be sharks in these waters, matey.

There might be moments when you don't like me very much. That's okay. I'm not here to coddle you—I am here to fight for you.

Let's go.

CHAPTER 1

You Don't Want What the Devil's Got in His Crock-Pot

In the Lusko household, the sound of the garage door opening is the starting gun for a flurry of activity. Tabasco, our miniature poodle and the only male in the house besides me, begins barking from his perch on the couch. At least one or two of my daughters hide somewhere in the house, and sometimes Clover, the youngest, barges out to greet me and carries my backpack inside. It's key that I finish my work before opening the garage door. I once made the mistake of initiating the routine before wrapping it up and ended up disappointing some little hearts. They had done their hiding, but I didn't do any seeking.

This tradition started when it was just Jennie and me living as newlyweds in an apartment in Albuquerque, New Mexico. We got a discount on the normal rate because it had a scenic view of the community Dumpster. "Look on the bright side," I told Jennie. "We won't have far to walk when we take out the trash!"

We gladly accepted the reduced price because it fit our budget. I was a youth pastor, and she worked as a waitress at Romano's Macaroni Grill, where she perfected both writing her name upside down with a crayon and singing "Happy Birthday" in Italian. Because she had mainly lunch shifts, I would usually arrive home from work after her. For some reason she began hiding from me, and I would have to find her. There weren't many places to look: the pantry, the linen closet, the spare room that doubled as an office. Her hiding place would change, but what happened when I found her did not. We were newlyweds, after all, and we couldn't keep our hands off each other. (Still can't.) It is somewhat ironic that once we had kids, our daughters adopted this game of hide-and-seek, as more likely than not, at least one of them was conceived as a result of it.

My other favorite thing about coming home is the smell that meets me when I walk in the door. Jennie does an absolutely wonderful job of creating an atmosphere, and she usually has candles lit, music playing, and something delicious cooking. In the winter, often something hot and bubbling has been cooking slowly in the Crock-Pot for hours: a delicious chili, a spicy Thai curry, or some hearty and filling shepherd's pie with ground turkey (instead of beef) and sweet potatoes.

I'm making you hungry, aren't I? As I write this I'm sitting in a hotel in downtown Los Angeles. It's 9:00 a.m., but I'm craving soup!

There is nothing quite like walking into a warm, cozy house, with a fire roaring, a puppy yipping, little girls screaming and running, candles dripping wax on the table, and something rich and savory simmering in the kitchen. Life is good.

When I was a teenager I always wanted to go out and do something. Staying at home was the worst. I pretty much feel the opposite these days. I've been out and done stuff. I'd much rather stay in. Plus I wear sweats as a uniform in my home, and no one is there to judge me. (Although it might have gotten a bit excessive: the other day I put a pair of jeans on, and my five-year-old daughter, Daisy, looked at me and said, "Are you preaching today? You only wear real pants on preaching days.")

That's what I want to talk to you about in this chapter, and to be honest, it's the reason I wrote this book. Not sweatpants—something cooking slowly in a Crock-Pot. It isn't a delicious home-cooked meal either. This Crock-Pot belongs to the devil, and trust me when I tell you that you don't want what he's got inside his electric cauldron. It smells delicious, and just the scent of it will drive you, like Edmund in the Chronicles of Narnia being offered Turkish delight, into a frenzy. But you need to know that Satan is slow cooking the death of your calling.

> You need to know that Satan is slow cooking the death of your calling.

WAY BACK WHEN

There was a steamy stew brewing for Esau. To understand what was at stake, we have to go all the way back to Esau's grandpa Abraham, one of the most famous dudes in the whole Bible. His nickname is the Father of Faith or just Father Abraham. Ironically, for someone who went down in history as a dad, old Abram (as his name was at the beginning of the story) and his wife, Sarai, had a really difficult time having kids. To make matters worse, the name Abram meant "exalted father." Imagine his embarrassment when introducing himself, as people constantly asked how many kids he had, only to learn he had none—in a culture that equated a barren womb with the judgment of God! That would be like having the unfortunate name Anthony Weiner and then being caught up in a sexting scandal.

Abram and Sarai grew old and eventually gave up on the idea of having a family. He accepted that his servant Eliezer was going to be the beneficiary of his considerable estate. Then God showed up with an amazing, ridiculous promise: "Abram, you and Sarai are going to have so many descendants that they will be more in number than the stars in the night sky. Out of your family will come great nations. Through those nations, kings will be born who will bless the whole world" (Genesis 15:2–5, 17:4–6, author's paraphrase). Eventually a messiah would come from Abraham's descendants, crush the head of the devil, and destroy death.

As insanely, improbably bizarre as it was to hear such a thing, Abram believed God on the spot, and God "accounted it to him for righteousness" (Genesis 15:6). In other words, God opened an umbrella called grace over Abram's life, and from that moment forward, not one drop of wrath would ever splash onto his skin. That's faith, by the way: triggering grace by taking God at his word. Latching onto the words that come from his mouth—no ifs, ands, or buts. In this ancient story, Abraham modeled for us what God has asked of us from the beginning: faith.

We mistakenly think that going to heaven is based on *doing* something, but it's based on *believing* something: God's promises. Author and pastor Jentezen Franklin put it this way: "You don't get good to get God, you get God to get good."[1] So it's not about what you can do; it's about you believing what God did and will do. Ephesians 2:8–9 tells us that "salvation is by grace through faith" (author's paraphrase). Abram's experience became the prototype for how we are saved today—by putting our faith and trust in Jesus.

I like to imagine that Abram went home, put on a little Drake in the tent, chilled a bottle of champagne, and surprised Sarai with some roses. As you do.

But they didn't have a baby.

Years went by. It seemed as if God had completely forgotten about them and failed to keep his word, but God again reminded Abram of his promise. God even went so far as to change Abram's name to Abraham, which means "father of many nations," and Sarai's name to Sarah.

At this point, Abraham was ninety-nine years old, and Sarah was about ninety. Speaking about it afterward, the book of Hebrews says God waited until Abraham's body was "as good as dead" (11:12). In case you are wondering, that's not a compliment. I don't imagine many Tinder profiles have that as a description:

My name is Tim. I am in banking. I like cooking and playing soccer, and my body is as good as dead. Swipe right for a good time . . .

But once the sitch was several levels beyond impossible, God intervened. Sidenote: it ain't over till it's over, but even when it is over, God can add time to the clock.

HAIRY AND HEEL-CATCHER

The stork finally showed up. It wasn't clean and tidy by any means; there was a lapse of faith when Abraham and Sarah had a baby with a surrogate, thinking God needed help. But he didn't. In God's perfect, impossible time, Abraham and Sarah conceived and named their baby boy Isaac, which is fitting because it means "laughter." I'm sure this geriatric couple got plenty of laughs as they pushed the stroller around when they weren't far from needing wheelchairs themselves.

Isaac grew up and married Rebekah, a wonderful girl with a nose ring. After Rebekah struggled with infertility for twenty years herself, she and Isaac finally got pregnant— only it was a buy-one-get-one-free deal, because she had twins. This is where it gets tricky and murky. There was a forked branch in the family tree. God's promise to Abraham was that through his seed all the people of the earth would be blessed (Genesis 12:3). After God made it clear his blessing was to go to Isaac and not Ishmael, it was easy to identify his chosen people. But now that Danny DeVito and Arnold Schwarzenegger were candidates for God's blessing, there was some question as to who would inherit it.

From an ancient historical perspective, the mantle should have gone to the firstborn. Whichever twin came out first would take the lion's share of Grandfather Abraham's promise into the future.

The due date finally arrived. First out was a hairy baby whom they named Esau (a creative name that, in the original Hebrew, means "hairy"). The second baby was born holding onto Chewbacca's foot, so they called him Heel-Catcher. We know him today as Jacob.

The two couldn't possibly have been more different: "Esau was a skillful hunter, a man of the field; but Jacob was a mild man, dwelling in tents" (Genesis 25:27). They were like Bass Pro Shop and Williams-Sonoma. Esau liked to cover himself in elk urine and go bow hunting. Jacob sat around customizing his Blue Apron orders and drinking espresso with his mom. They didn't have a whole lot in common—except that they were vying for their father's attention.

You won't believe what happened next.

Genesis 25:29–30 says, "Now Jacob cooked a stew; and Esau came in from the field, and he was weary. And Esau said to Jacob, 'Please feed me with that same red stew, for I am weary.'" The men had spent the afternoon each doing what each liked best—Esau had tried to kill wild animals, and Jacob had loafed around the house, tweeting and trying out a new recipe for bean soup that he had found on Pinterest. When Esau arrived in the tent exhausted and starving, the whole place smelled amazing because of this big, bubbling pot of stew his homebody brother was cooking. The scene was like one from Looney Tunes: the aroma from the stove reached out to grab Esau by the nostrils, and he floated across the room absolutely intoxicated by the smell.

I can just imagine Jacob pulling a tray of steaming

biscuits out of the oven in front of a drooling Esau and saying matter-of-factly, "Sell me your birthright as of this day" (Genesis 25:31).

I should pause right here and acknowledge that "birthright" doesn't exactly ring a bell in our day, but four thousand years ago, it was a huge deal. As the name suggests, the birthright belonged to the firstborn male, and it gave him three things:

1. A double portion of the inheritance. It caused the firstborn to be seen in the will as though he were two people. So if there were two sons, the firstborn would get two-thirds of the estate and the sibling would get one-third.

2. A leadership role. The firstborn became the chief executive officer of the family business. In the event of a disagreement in how things should be run or done, he had the deciding vote, and his brothers and sisters had to defer to him.

3. Last, and most significantly, a spiritual blessing. He acted as the priest of the home. In Abraham's family, this would also mean receiving the promise from God and propagating his chosen people and ultimately the Messiah.

In other words, having the birthright was a really, really big deal. And because he was born first, it was Esau's. No one could pry it from his fingers.

Keep that in mind as you picture Jacob saying, "If you give me your birthright, I'll totally let you have some of my stew." I'm sure his proposition seems as ridiculous to you as it seems to me. It's obviously not a good deal. (By the way, it's always easy to know how other people should respond to their temptations because we aren't the ones standing there light-headed and with low blood sugar, smelling the stew on the fire.)

Esau should have been outraged by this offer. He ought to have swiped left so fast it would have made Jacob's head spin. He should have thrown his hands up in the air and said, "Are you kidding me? You want me to trade all that God wants to do in my life, and all that he has promised to do through me generations from now, for a bowl of stew?"

I heard pastor Andy Stanley preach on this text once. He said that if he could have called a time-out, he would have sat Esau down and explained to him that from that moment forward, God would introduce himself to ultra-significant people, such as Moses, as "the God of Abraham, Isaac, and Esau"—but if Esau made this deal with his brother, the saying would become "I am the God of Abraham, Isaac, and Jacob."[2] God always gives us a way of escape when we are tempted. The key is to slow down. You can't see the escape route as well when you are hauling.

But Esau took no time to think about introductions or chosen people or double portions. All he could think about was how delicious that stew would taste as it passed briefly through his mouth: "And Esau said, 'Look, I am about to die; so what is this birthright to me?'" (Genesis 25:32). Translation: "I'm starving *now* and will probably die if I don't eat this food, so what good is a promise of what I might get *someday*?"

Let's be clear about something: Esau wasn't starving to death. Maybe he was really, really hungry, but he had walked in there, hadn't he? He'd said "please." Esau's response is hyperbole at its finest. But in that moment, nothing mattered to him more than having a full stomach.

THE POINT OF NO RETURN

Red pill, blue pill. Swipe left, swipe right. Two options were on the table: Would you like this meal right now, or would you like to see God do great things through your life down the road? Genesis 25:33–34 says,

> Then Jacob said, "Swear to me as of this day."
> So he swore to him, and sold his birthright to Jacob. And Jacob gave Esau bread and stew of lentils; then he ate and drank, arose, and went his way. Thus Esau despised his birthright.

Just like that.

Esau chose the stew. He traded his calling for a can of Campbell's. He gave up his inheritance for something that made him feel good for an evening. He could have been a part of a chain of events that led to Christ coming to the world, but he wrote himself out of the story.

It seems that Esau was a man of intense physical desires. He did whatever he felt like doing, no matter what, and it kept him from reaching his potential. Like Paul warned the church at Philippi, Esau's god was his belly, and it led to destruction (Philippians 3:19). His highest good was to feel good.

But the next morning, he was hungry again. Within twenty-four hours he had digested and eliminated the meal he just had to have. In the end, he lost everything.

Because hindsight is twenty-twenty, and the fog has cleared and the dust has settled, you and I can sit here shaking our heads at Esau for being so shortsighted. A better use of our time would be for me to tell you that somewhere, in some kitchen, there is a big, simmering pot of stew that the devil will serve up to you at just the right time—and it will be just as tempting to you as Esau's was to him. When that day comes, whatever is being asked of you in return for a taste will seem so far off and uncertain that all you'll be able to think of is how delicious and happy the stew will make you in that moment. If you're not careful, and if you don't keep a cool head, you'll be tempted to take a bite.

WATCH OUT FOR THE ESAU SYNDROME

Trust me when I say this: you don't want what the devil's got in his Crock-Pot, where he's slow-cooking the death of God's highest and best plans for your life. Satan knows what you desperately need to understand: desires can keep you from your destiny. That's why Scripture warns us, "Watch out for the Esau syndrome: trading away God's lifelong gift in order to satisfy a short-term appetite. You well know how Esau later regretted that impulsive act and wanted God's blessing—but by then it was too late, tears or no tears" (Hebrews 12:14–17 THE MESSAGE).

You and I are joking if we think we are immune to this temptation. In fact, instant gratification is the norm in the world today. People are lovers of pleasure, and they want it now.

We have all sorts of desires—the desire to eat, the desire to have sex, the desire to be liked, the desire to win, the desire to prosper and be rich, the desire to be known. In and of themselves, none of these desires are bad; in fact they're all God-given. However, since Adam and Eve bit into the banned fruit, sin has influenced our desires. Like them, we can satisfy good desires in the wrong way.

A powerful warning is tucked into a book Jesus' little brother James wrote: "Each one is tempted when he is drawn away by his own desires and enticed. Then, when desire has conceived, it gives birth to sin; and sin, when it is full-grown, brings forth death" (James 1:14–15). When you sneak a sip from a Crock-Pot, you move away from God's best for your life:

- the beautiful, fulfilling, and selfless intimacy he has destined for your marriage,
- the life-giving and healthy home your kids are supposed to grow up in,
- the remarkable, innovative, and creative things God wants to do through your ministry or your business,
- and the souls you are meant to reach.

The calling God has on your life can be silenced by the desire to feel good in the moment. The desire for sex can cause you to look at porn or have an affair that will wreck your home, make your kids hate you, and discredit your witness. The desire to succeed in business can cause you to cut corners and make unethical decisions, give people a bad impression of Jesus-followers, and possibly cost you your job or put you in prison. You can end up trading what God wants to give you for a bowl of stew.

The *ultimate* for the *instant*.

Forever can be eclipsed by *for a moment*.

Your physical desires can derail your destiny, if you let them. Because if you don't understand your calling, you'll undervalue it.

One of my favorite TV shows is *Shark Tank*. Aspiring entrepreneurs or inventors pitch their businesses or products to a group of billionaire investors in order to get venture capital. They explain why their new potato peeler, light bulb, or grass-cutting device deserves an investment, and then they haggle over the terms.

As the investors—the "sharks"—respond to the opportunity to own a piece of an entrepreneur's company, they often say something like, "Your valuation of your business is too high. You're saying your company is worth a million dollars. I'll offer you a hundred thousand dollars for fifty percent ownership, because your company is really worth only two hundred thousand dollars." Then the entrepreneur either agrees with that value and accepts the offer or rejects it.

The sharks will almost always try to undervalue the company and get it for a deal. Their goal is to own as much as they can for as little as possible. There is one shark who calls himself Mr. Wonderful. He is notorious for being a scoundrel and says all kinds of loving things like, "You're dead to me," and, "You're going to get crushed like the cockroach that you are." He cares about only the money and is ruthlessly vocal about his desire to get more of it at all costs. He will not only attack those entrepreneurs in the tank but even turn on his fellow sharks.

The devil works in the same way. He is the ultimate predator. He'll always try to rip you off by offering you much less than you're worth. If you let him, he will get you to trade all your spiritual power for a bowl of SpaghettiOs. And if you don't understand your true worth, you will settle.

Hear me loud and clear: you might feel ordinary or common, but you're not. You matter more than you know. If you are a believer in Jesus, you are a son or daughter of the King of all kings, saved by God's Son and sealed with his Holy Spirit. Your name is already on an assigned seat in heaven. As God's child, you have a birthright and an inheritance, and you are a named beneficiary in his living will. In other words, if God has it, you have it!

You are destined to rule and reign with Christ, to overcome and sit with him on his throne one day. And in the meantime, he wants you to take part in the family business—to live on earth as it is in heaven so that it may be below as it is above.

Maybe you've seen angry, red-faced preachers wag their fingers in your face and yell about the commandments you've broken, and so you don't understand how much God loves you. If so, let me tell you a little bit about how *very* much God loves you. Yes, you—the person holding this book and reading these words.

He has great plans for you.

He intends for you to flourish and thrive.

He wants to give you a future full of hope.

He wants your marriage to be a source of joy and fun.

He wants you to have amazing sex.

He wants your sons to "be as plants grown up in their youth";

your daughters to "be as pillars, sculptured in palace style";

and your children to be arrows in the hand of a warrior shot out.

(I'm not making this stuff up; check out Jeremiah 29:11, Psalm 144:12, Psalm 127:4, and the entire Song of Solomon.)

He is a fisherman, and he caught you for a purpose. He didn't get stuck with you; he specifically went out looking for you, and through your life, he wants to do exceedingly abundantly above all that you could ask or think (Ephesians 3:20).

I intentionally belabor this point because the easiest way to get ripped off is to not understand the power of your potential.

The devil loves to make you insecure about your calling. He tries to persuade you that God wouldn't want to use you, in the hopes that you'll leave the shark tank having given your entire company away to Mr. Wonderful in a terrible deal that makes him rich while you work your fingers to the bone. The devil is a shark who never sleeps. He knows that if you are a believer, he can't take you to hell; but if you let him, he *will* keep you from living for heaven. If you are in Christ, you have already crossed over the Red Sea and left Egypt, so his goal is to keep you from entering into the promised land. (Translation: You are at Disneyland with a Park Hopper ticket, but it's up to you how many rides you go on before the park closes. The devil wants you to keep spinning in the teacups and riding It's a Small World so you won't notice the Matterhorn. He definitely doesn't want you setting foot on Space Mountain. The price of your ticket has been paid in full, so I say you milk it for all it's worth!)

> He knows that if you are a believer, he can't take you to hell; but if you let him, he *will* keep you from living for heaven.

This is a book about sex, dating, marriage, and romance. But it's also about so much more than that. I didn't carve out the time to write it so I can tell you, "Don't sin." That's not what causes my heart to race as I type these words and imagine you reading them. The message that fills my bones with fire is that God wants you to rise up, take your place, and change the world. It's your calling, and you were born for this. But full disclosure: it's not going to happen apart from following God's plans for your life—and that includes your love life.

Too often sex is treated as an end unto itself, but all the pieces of our lives should be viewed as part of something more. This concept of looking for something beyond the mundane or trying to find a metanarrative is probably something you would expect to hear from a pastor, but it's also advice the CEO of one of the biggest companies on earth included in his memoir. Nike cofounder Phil Knight wrote, "I'd tell men and women in their midtwenties not to settle for a job or a profession or even a career. Seek a calling. Even if you don't know what that means, seek it. If you're following your calling, the fatigue will be easier to bear, the disappointments will be fuel, the highs will be like nothing you've ever felt."[3]

Pulled from the bigger context, God's plan for sex and romance isn't going to be any fun. It will actually suck sometimes. But when you think follow-through, you aren't stopping at the ball; you are hitting past it and unlocking great power along the way.

That's why the devil wants so badly to get you to trade all your spiritual power for a casual encounter—for you to think you can "hit it and quit it" but then not be transformed by the action. And if you're trapped in a prison of porn addiction, you won't be out on the battlefield, defeating the kingdom of darkness.

Don't you dare trade your calling for something that's one-and-done. Don't let the devil determine the value of your life for you. He's a liar! He will whisper that sleeping with someone will make you feel loved—but you are already loved by an almighty God. He will whisper that looking at porn is normal, harmless, and will satisfy—but you will be hungry again. He will whisper that you are missing out by not doing what your friends are doing—and that one's true! By following God's plan you are missing out on heartache, regret, guilt, and a whole lot of sadness.

When Chef Boyardee calls, let it go to voice mail.

Now yells louder, but *later* lasts longer.

Instead, decide that when he tempts you, you're going to throw the stew off the table. *Now* yells louder, but *later* lasts longer. Resolve to stand up and take the place in the kingdom of God that you were born to inherit.

CHAPTER 2

The Problem with Pineapples

When was the last time you bought a pineapple? Do you remember how much you paid for it? Most fruit in the grocery store is sold by the pound, which means you have to hunt for a scale to figure out exactly how much it will cost. This is one of several bizarre grocery store rituals. For instance, what's up with the bathroom always being hidden in the most inconvenient spot, and the casino-like lack of windows or clocks? I'm convinced grocery stores are designed to make you feel lost, disoriented, and—of course—hungry.

I have never successfully made it out of a grocery store without feeling frustrated. Jennie has learned never to send me to the market without a very specific list, because she knows that if she gives me verbal instructions, I'll come home with nothing she asked for and a look of confusion about why I went there in the first place. Even with a list, I'm admittedly out of my depth. I end up making inefficient laps around the store, because I work my way through the list from top to bottom, inevitably making trips back and forth to get items in aisles where I've already been. I'm just so focused on what Jennie has asked me to get, and I don't want to blow it. *Chili powder, chili powder, chili powder,* I think, and then I'm like, *children's allergy medicine, children's allergy medicine.* . . . Inevitably my movements are more crisscross than they are methodical.

Then there are the curious notes she's added. She will write things like "laundry detergent" and then add beside it, "the most natural you can find." I am thinking to myself, *What a hippie! Natural is washing them in a stream. I want something man-made, in a lab. Something with added chemicals and scrubbing bubbles in exchange for my hardearned dollars.* Jennie will list "kale, parsley, cilantro, and spinach," but then she'll note that the spinach has to be organic. Now I'm eyeing vegetables suspiciously: *How wild are you?* Recently I spent much longer than I care to admit standing in front of a cooler and trying to figure out which butter comes from grass-fed cows. I had so many questions, starting with, *What else can they feed a cow, and why does that even matter?*

There are, of course, other Grocery Store Problems, such as choosing a checkout line. I am prone to major indecision in those moments. Some would say to pick the shortest one, but that's a rookie mistake: length can be deceiving. You could choose a short line behind a coupon-clipping, checkwriting Chatty Cathy and be there until your next birthday. I live for the moment when a new checkout line is opened. Not when an employee broadcasts, "Lane 7 is now open" over the loud speakers—that's code for "Soccer moms, start your engines!" I'm talking about that rare occasion when a sweet angel in the disguise of a clerk comes up from behind, taps you on the shoulder, tells you, "I can take care of you over here," and leads you to an open register. That's like meeting a unicorn with rainbows shooting out of its eyes.

For a very long time, every time I checked out at the grocery store, the clerk would say to me, "Thank you and have a nice day, Mr. Robinson!" And I would thank the clerk and walk away laughing. This started when I didn't have a loyalty card to present upon checkout and the clerk said I could give my phone number instead. I tried my cell phone number and my wife's. No dice. I tried the number for the home phone we used to have before realizing there was absolutely no purpose in having a home phone. Nada. Finally I tried an old cell phone number from ten years ago that I somehow still remembered—even though there was absolutely no way I had hooked up a frequent shopping card at that stage of my life. I fed the now fatigued cashier the number and voilà! It worked. I looked smugly at the exasperated line behind me as though to say, *Nailed it! Fourth time's the charm.* It then became endlessly amusing to me to use that number and get the discount and live a secret life—if only for a moment.

Once, when Jennie was with me at the market, she tried to hand her loyalty card to me to use. I assured her it wasn't necessary, gave the old number, and when she heard me greeted as "Mr. Robinson," I shot her a look to say, "Don't blow this for me." I thought I was so clever because of all the savings I had racked up without being a member and was thoroughly pleased with myself—until she burst my bubble by telling me that the points for the store's program give you a discount for buying gas at the grocer's gas station, and none of my purchases had gone to our account. I looked blankly at her and thought of the man with my old cell phone number, probably living on a private island, rejoicing at all the unexpected free gas that had mysteriously fallen from the heavens. Well played, Mr. Robinson, well played.

Back to pineapples. You probably only paid a few bucks for one, right? Did you know that they used to be so expensive and highly sought after that only the extraordinarily wealthy could stand a chance of getting one? No joke. When pineapples arrived in Europe after Christopher Columbus first discovered them in the New World, people were so intrigued by this fruit that looked like a pinecone but was juicy like an apple (thus the name *pineapple*) that they became a symbol of luxury and privilege. There was a point in time when having a taste of pineapple would have been the highlight of a person's life.[1]

At its peak, a pineapple sold for as much as eight thousand dollars in today's currency.[2] Instead of eating it, people would display the fruit until it rotted.[3] They would even have viewing parties! Can you imagine people coming to your home just to sit around and stare at a piece of fruit? Hard to believe, but it's true. Pineapples also appear in architecture and design as a thing of beauty. For example, St. Paul's Cathedral in London has an enormous golden pineapple on its south tower.

Imagine if you could bring someone from the 1500s or 1600s to an Albertson's to see piles of $2.99 pineapples sitting between the watermelons and mangos, as customers nonchalantly speared samples with toothpicks from a little plastic case on a pedestal while milling about the produce section. Your time-traveling visitor would flip out!

Why doesn't anyone care about pineapples today? Why aren't they protected or celebrated? They're easy to come by, so their value has been greatly diminished. The advance of the steamship and the development of pineapple plantations made them widely available and thus less special. That's the problem with pineapples: it's easy to take for granted what you have a lot of. Familiarity breeds contempt, as the adage goes. One writer observed, "It still tastes exactly the same. But now, the pineapple is one of the world's least glamorous fruits. The pineapple itself has not changed; only our attitude to it has."[4]

WATER EVERYWHERE AND NOT A DROP TO DRINK

I wonder if that's an appropriate analogy for what has happened to sex. It was meant to be something rare and exotic that we would only ever experience in one very specific context. Think for a moment how you would feel if you had sex with only one person your entire life, if you were naked with only that one person. Imagine that the gift of knowing you intimately, out of all the billions of people on the earth, belonged to just that one special someone. That would make sex a pretty spectacular, noteworthy thing, wouldn't it? A treasure to be valued. The opposite of common. That's the way God designed it to be.

Adam knew his wife, and they were naked and not ashamed. He was the only one using her Safeway card to get rewards at the pumps. Eve didn't compare Adam's performance to other men she had been with, and Adam didn't struggle to suppress mental images of other women he had seen on the Internet. Neither was concerned that the other would wake up with an unexplained rash because of an STD contracted from a previous partner. All they knew was each other—and it was very good.

Proverbs 5:16 warns, "Drink water from your own well; don't let it be dispersed in the streets" (author's paraphrase). Solomon praised his bride in the Song of Solomon as a garden enclosed—closed off to trespassers and open only to him (4:12). He belonged to a club so exclusive that it only had one member.

Some people compare premarital sex to test-driving a car. They're concerned about "buying without trying"—getting into a marriage without experience with or knowledge about what they're committing to. But when you have all the sex you want, anywhere you want, with whomever you want, there's nothing sacred or special about it. The more people you choose to have sex with, the less the experience means. Easy come easy go. Common is the opposite of special. Beached fish don't die because there isn't enough oxygen, but because there is too much. Eventually sex becomes only a shadow of what it was meant to be. Sex itself has not changed; only our attitudes toward it have.

Julia A'Bell of Hillsong Church once offered advice on time management: "If you grow your no, God can bless your yes." It struck me when I heard it because, as many people do, I tend to overcommit. Every new commitment dilutes the effectiveness of what I have already committed to. Therefore *no* is what gives *yes* its power. Time is a zero-sum affair; there's only so much to go around. If you say yes to enough trivial things, what's most important in your life will have to foot the bill.

When it comes to sex, I wonder if it's not what we say yes to that's the problem, but rather what we aren't saying no to. If we want God to bless our "I dos," perhaps the solution is increasing our "I won'ts" before marriage begins, so that we never say, "I don't."

HUNGER LOWERS YOUR STANDARDS

Candy corn Oreos, peanut butter M&M's, Star Wars–branded Yoda-edition Lucky Charms, Ben & Jerry's cookie dough ice cream: these are things I have purchased after walking into a Safeway hungry—things I wouldn't have bought if I'd walked in with a stomach full of chicken breast and broccoli. For me, a thirty-four-year-old with a slowing metabolism, the problem is that these treats

> If we want God to bless our "I dos," perhaps the solution is increasing our "I won'ts" before marriage begins, so that we never say, "I don't."

are delicious on the lips and then a disaster on my hips. Lovely on the eyes, not so much on the thighs. I also have a huge problem not eating my kids' leftover chicken fingers and French fries. "I don't want them to go to waste," I rationalize. In saner moments I respond to myself, "Better in the waste than on your waist!" The struggle is real. I have a love-hate relationship with food—I love junk food and hate eating healthy. You know what else I hate, though? My gut muffin-topping over my low-rise jeans. Curse you, chips and salsa.

It has taken me a while, but I've realized that I'm safer when my stomach is full of good things. I keep Quest bars, almonds, and protein shakes around me at all times, so I always have something on hand to help me ward off temptation. I believe God wants you to be a picky eater, to be careful and selective about what you bring into your heart and into your life. The devil knows that hunger is the single greatest way to outmaneuver a picky eater. When you are hungry, you are much less guarded about what you eat.

That's why the devil, when he tempted Jesus in the wilderness, came when he did: "And when He had fasted forty days and forty nights, *afterward He was hungry.* Now when the tempter came to Him, he said, 'If You are the Son of God, command that these stones become bread'" (Matthew 4:2–3, emphasis added).

When you fast for an extended period of time, the first few days are the hardest. After that your headaches and hunger start to go away. Your stomach shrinks, and your body figures out how to survive. You feel weak, but you don't have the same pain. I've found that by day five of a fast, I start feeling pretty good.

I've never fasted long enough to find out, but I've read that your hunger pains don't come back until you begin to starve. It's your body's way of sending out an SOS. After nearly six weeks, that is surely what Jesus was experiencing. And the devil had no problem exploiting Jesus' hunger by talking about bread. Carbs: that's more than anyone can bear! *The Message* presents the scene vividly: "[The fast] left him, of course, in a state of extreme hunger, which the Devil took advantage of in the first test: 'Since you are God's Son, speak the word that will turn these stones into loaves of bread'" (Matthew 4:2–3). Satan knew that after forty days, even rocks would look good!

Why do you think Jacob propositioned Esau when he was starving? He didn't bring the question up at breakfast, right after his older brother had eaten: "Hey, would you like to sell me your birthright for stew?" Esau would have given him a wedgie! Instead, Jacob made the offer when Esau was hungry because he couldn't see clearly on an empty stomach. Neither can you.

The devil will wait until you're run down to bring you temptation that promises relief. Imagine you're feeling lonely and lovesick from heartbreak when you bump into your ex. You think, *What are the odds?* but the next thing you know . . . *Bam!* Booty call! Even though you know you shouldn't, the opportunity to hook up will seem appealing, almost as though it were an answer to prayer.

The devil has tremendous timing.

He knows just when to strike. When you are tired,

The devil will wait until you're run down to bring you temptation that promises relief.

when you have been fired, when you get into a fight with your spouse. That's when he'll bait the hook with comfort sin. Tinder notifications will chirp. A sketchy show will appear on TV or in your Netflix recommendations. An innocent hashtag you click will take you to a skanky photo. You'll think, *I deserve this. This will make me feel better. This will cheer me up.*

It might—for a little while. But then it will make you feel worse—a lot worse!

You have to anticipate the attack.

Put up your guard when you are weak.

When you are run down.

When you are having a bad day, or just got bad news, or are in a bad mood.

And especially . . . when you are hungry.

Say to yourself, *I am more susceptible to the enemy right now.* Raise the security alert level from orange to red. Be extra cautious with what comes your way. Be suspicious about all incoming communication.

You need to be on guard against hunger whether you are married or single. First Corinthians 7:5 advises wives and husbands not to cut each other off from sex, except for defined periods of prayer and fasting; otherwise, it is begging the devil to come between you. If you are not making it your goal to meet your spouse's need for sex within the godly, healthy parameters of your relationship, you are sending him or her out hungrier than necessary and causing any temptations that might come along to be that much more alluring.

If you're single, sexual temptation is everywhere. You can't get away from it. The hunger for sex isn't a bad thing; it's just not yet time to satiate that hunger. God has something so much better for you than what you would settle for right now. He wants you to wait to glue your soul to the one with whom you will spend your life, grow old, and die.

It's easier to lower your standards when you're hungry. Just as you counteract hunger for food with a full stomach, you can counteract hunger for sex with a full heart. The writer of Psalm 119:11 sang, "Your word I have hidden in my heart, / That I might not sin against You." How different temptation looks when you eat the bread of life and drink the living water before going out into the world to face the day. Developing a relationship with Jesus through God's Word, the Bible, fills your heart and clears your head. Then when temptations show up, you are able to see their true price tags, the shining hooks under the bait. You'll think, *Why would I want to give in to temptation when it would dull my love for Christ, compromise my strength, steal from my spiritual reward, and keep me from doing God's will?*

You won't want a mouthful of rocks because you are satisfied

> Fill your heart by doing God's will, and you won't have room for lesser things.

doing the will of him who sent you. Fill your heart by doing God's will, and you won't have room for lesser things.

God's got the perfect pineapple prepared just for you, Mr. Robinson, and if you play your cards right, a gas reward too.

CHAPTER 3

Scars Mean Sex

Twice a year my television viewing spikes: during the Tour de France and during Shark Week. One is the most grueling athletic event on earth, a bike race stretching more than two thousand miles up and down mountains so steep you'll get a nosebleed from just watching the bikers climb them; the other is a week of programming on the Discovery Channel dedicated to those mysterious, beautiful creatures with teeth and fins called sharks.

I love sharks. I have been obsessed with (and somewhat terrified by) those stealthy, living torpedoes all my life. Whenever we would go swimming, my father would do this thing he called *shark dad*. He would put a hand on his forehead, like a dorsal fin, and sneak up on us in the pool; then we would try to get away from him before he could attack us. I have continued the tradition with my girls, and I even have a tattoo of a great white shark in honor of my dad.

My dad also got me into road biking. I find it hypnotizing: the rhythmic whir of the moving pedals, the peloton swarming like angry bees through a roundabout, the energy of hundreds of thousands of fans on the sides of the roads—in some cases for days—hoping to glimpse these men playing chess on bicycles at speeds up to eighty miles per hour.

Needless to say, both the Tour de France and Shark Week have my undivided attention, but in the summer of 2015, the two worlds collided.

Typically Shark Week airs in August, and the Tour de France (hereafter to be referred to as *Le Tour*) happens in July. But for some reason, the Discovery Channel moved the 2015 Shark Week to July, smack dab in the middle of Le Tour.

I didn't know what to do. Watching a professional bike race takes commitment. The TV coverage of it lasts three to five hours a day for about three weeks. It's not for the faint of heart. Fortunately, because of the time difference, the race starts at 4:00 a.m. where I live and doesn't cut into my workday. I just get up early and have it on in the quiet pre-sunrise hours.

The rest of my family is usually awake by the time the racers are approaching the stage's finish line, and I fill them in on what they missed. Then I blast the volume for the final few minutes to the finish. My girls' favorite part is the conferring of the awards that takes place immediately after each stage. Race organizers give a polka-dotted jersey to the king of the mountain (the winner of the most points from the mountain stages), a green jersey to the best sprinter, and the coveted yellow jersey to the overall leader of the race.

Shark Week is a more casual viewing experience. We usually put it on in the background throughout the week, often with the volume muted, and in the evenings we watch one of the new programs—*Air Jaws 15* or whatever it is.

When Le Tour and Shark Week collided, I would bounce back and forth between the two, resulting in what we called Le Shark Week. My dreams were filled with hammerhead sharks attacking cyclists trying to summit Alpe d'Huez. May it never happen again.

Watching them simultaneously, I realized that the disparate events had something in common: carnage. The best (and worst) parts of Shark Week are the stories of shark attacks: a man on a beach lifts his pant leg to show where a tiger shark chewed off part of his calf muscle. Interestingly, the best (and worst) parts of professional cycling are the crashes. The prerace coverage inevitably includes a retired cyclist lifting his sleeve, telling the story of the crash of '97 when the road took the skin off his arm. Mark Cavendish, the "Manx Missile," crashed and broke his collarbone right in front of me when I attended Le Tour. And if you've never seen an entire peloton go down, please go to YouTube right now and search for "Tour de France crash montage." It is gnarly. If you road bike, you know the adage: it's not *if* you crash; it's *when*.

In the adrenaline-soaked mixture of aquatics and athletics, one of the programs we watched—*Island of the Mega Shark*[1]—really caught my attention. On screen were giant fourteen-foot white sharks that were scarred on their backs and sides. The narrator claimed, "There are definitely sexually mature females here." I wondered how on earth he knew this. Reading my mind, the narrator continued, "Their sides are a battleground of scars, and those scars mean sex. Males have to hold on somehow." Consequently, females who are sexually mature have scars on their sides and gills. Fortunately, for this very reason, a female shark's skin is twice as thick as that of a male.

I paused the show. I was no longer thinking about the yellow jersey or the scariest fish in the ocean. I pulled out my phone to write those three words in a new text document in Evernote: *scars mean sex.*

My mind was racing, thinking about the people in my life with emotional scar tissue—some healed and healthy, others infected and ugly. And in person after person after person, sex was the common denominator:

The friend whose marriage blew up after an affair. Scar.

The mother who discovered her son's sexting. Scar.

The man who got in a car accident on the way home from a visit to a prostitute, revealing the unfaithfulness that would have otherwise gone undetected. Scar.

The buddy who was given HIV by a girlfriend who knew she had it but didn't want to suffer alone. Scar.

The teenager whose life was a living hell because of naked pictures she sent to one person that ended up spread all over school. Scar.

The child who was molested by a family friend. Scar.

The family that disintegrated after the father's sexual addiction was exposed. Scar.

The young, sweet girl who was sexually assaulted by a stranger in a parking lot. Scar.

And the pastor who was exposed to pornography in junior high and fought a secret, smoldering obsession with it for years, making it difficult to honor women or myself. That's *my* scar.

Road rash left behind as evidence of a crash. Gaping wounds where there was once muscle. Scars mean sex.

Rape is at epidemic levels in the United States today. Meg Meeker noted in her book *Strong Fathers, Strong Daughters*, "11.9 percent of females will experience forced intercourse in their lives."[2] And a horrific 20 percent of women in college are sexually assaulted by the time they get out of university.[3] That's one out of five women going off to college who will be attacked, who will have had something precious taken from them.

A staggering number of children are sexually molested by predators: one out of four girls and one out of six boys.[4] Many of those who commit these crimes are abuse victims themselves. It doesn't excuse their actions, but it explains them. Hurt people hurt people.

DEEPER THAN SKIN

Why do the effects of sexual trauma linger like festering wounds that haven't been cleaned? If left untreated, why does sexual abuse shape a life?[5] Why can't you just "move on and get over it" without the pain coming back to haunt you? Perhaps it is for the simple reason that, contrary to what our culture preaches, sex is much more than a physical activity.

When I was in high school, a shocking but popular song by a band called Bloodhound Gang extolled the effects of evolution on sexual reproduction. The idea of the catchy chorus was that sex should be experienced the way animals enjoy it on programs you can see on networks such as National Geographic or Discovery. (I am wording this very carefully to avoid actually quoting the lyrics, because if I do my editor is going to flag this in her review and tell me it will be too expensive and difficult to obtain permission to quote them here. I will tell you that *channel* and *mammal* were rhymed.)

The song was a proclamation of emancipation. Because you and I are mammals, and sex is only a biological experience, we should "do it" at will. We should throw off any constraint or caution and get busy as we feel like it. Bite the back of any shark in sight and start humping.

This song was an admittedly blunt—but refreshingly honest—articulation of the secular perspective on sexuality: just like eating or drinking, sex is merely the function of an appetite we developed out of necessity in order for our species to survive. So as long as you take steps to curtail unwanted reproduction and minimize the spread of infectious diseases, you should feel entitled to enjoy it as you see fit, free from consequences. If the sex you are having is safe and consensual, who's to say what is wrong or right? Swipe left, swipe right, swipe any way you want—we're all free to do whatever we feel like doing. Of course, if you carry this mammalian perspective out to its furthest conclusion, who is to say that any sexual choices are out of bounds? No one would judge a grizzly bear by human standards of what is illegal or taboo. That's just how it is on the Discovery Channel. What biological benefit is there in evolving a conscience?

Today's secular perspective of sexuality is not just about the sex drive, but about letting sex drive. The highest good is to feel good. Impulse control is not a hot commodity. We don't want to bow the knee of our sexuality to heaven and humbly say, "Thy will be done." We would rather claim there is no God so we can say, "My will be done."

I was in a Soul Cycle spin class where the instructor kept shouting motivational statements to get us to dig deeper. One thing that she repeated several times stuck out to me. She kept saying, "Trust your instincts. They will never steer you wrong." That's precisely what animals do.

Deep down we know we are not animals. No one flinches when one animal hurts another; they are just "trusting their instincts." But when we see people act like animals, we are appalled.

Today's secular perspective of sexuality is not just about the sex drive, but about letting sex drive.

An Old Testament story about a man named Amnon illustrates what happens when you let sex drive your life: it will steer you wrong. Amnon was so full of sexual desire for his half-sister Tamar that he made himself sick thinking about her. A friend helped him scheme to be alone with her, and Amnon forced himself on her. Amnon was obsessed with Tamar right up until he had her—and then he wanted nothing to do with her. The Bible captures the moment when his "love" for her showed its true colors: "Then Amnon hated her exceedingly, so that the hatred with which he hated her was greater than the love with which he had loved her. And Amnon said to her, 'Arise, be gone!'" (2 Samuel 13:15).

In truth Amnon never loved Tamar at all. Love gives and doesn't take. Love is not forceful. Love is patient and selfless; it causes you to seek the highest good for the object of your affection, not for yourself.

The reactions you and I feel as we read about Amnon's treatment of Tamar is telling. As a father to four daughters, the story makes my blood boil. Amnon violated Tamar and deprived her of her sexual innocence. He took something that was not for him. I want to hire Jax and the rest of the Sons of Anarchy to beat him until he bleeds from his eyes and ears. Don't you have a similar reaction?

But why does rape make you see red? In truth, all Amnon did was behave like the animals on the Discovery Channel. Our consciences and our humanity betray us. We know better because we have been given more.

In truth, the scars Amnon inflicted on Tamar were not the only ones in the story. They were matched by the ones Amnon inflicted upon himself, deep down inside his own soul. Why? Because sex is more than just a physical activity.

It's more than just the sum of its parts. It engages you on the deepest possible levels: body, soul, spirit, and mind.

CHASING TWO RABBITS

It's so important that you get this. Maybe right now you're experimenting or sleeping around—maybe not a lot, just a little—and you plan to stop. You want to sow your wild oats now, and then move on to the happy family, the white picket fence, 2.5 kids, and the awesome marriage that lasts until death do you part. You think you can have the best of both worlds.

I think deep down we all want to do whatever we want (now) and to have what God wants (later).

That's not how it works.

You can't just flip a switch and undo what you have done, who you have become. When the cake is eaten, it's eaten. You can't eat it and still have it. The problem with chasing two rabbits is you will lose them both.

Every time you have sex with someone, it changes you—and extramarital sex shreds you up on the inside. When we engage in sex outside of God's plan, it can make us unable to enjoy it inside his plan.

Paul put it this way:

> Do you not know that your bodies are members of Christ? Shall I then take the members of Christ and make them members of a harlot? Certainly not! Or do you not know that he who is joined to a harlot is one body with her? For "the two," He says, "shall become one flesh." But he who is joined to the Lord is one spirit with Him.
>
> Flee sexual immorality. Every sin that a man does is outside the body, but he who commits sexual immorality sins against his own body. (1 Corinthians 6:15–18)

Like any other sin, sexual sin was paid for when Jesus' blood trickled down the cross. Like all sin, sexual sin is forgivable. But unlike some other sins, it's also a sin against yourself. That means that even if you don't get an STD or face a pregnancy, sex still affects you in a significant way. My friend Louie Giglio, pastor of Passion City Church in Atlanta, captured this reality perfectly when he said, in response to the notion of "safe sex" outside of God's plan, "They don't make a condom that can fit over your soul."[6]

I understand that this is a lot to swallow, and maybe you're thinking, *I need a chapter and verse for that.* Check this out: "There's more to sex than mere skin on skin. Sex is as much spiritual mystery as physical fact" (1 Corinthians 6:16 THE MESSAGE). It changes who you are—and you can't unscramble those eggs. You can't go through your single years bonding to partners and then ripping apart over and over again, and then all of a sudden be a different person when you get married. There will be scars.

The more times you pull up a Post-it note and attempt to restick it, the less powerful the adhesive becomes. Like a frequently moved Post-it note, sexuality loses its stickiness over time. Sex is meant to glue two people together for a lifetime: "A man shall leave his father and mother and be joined to his wife, and they shall become one flesh" (Genesis 2:24). In Hebrew, the word translated "joined" means "to be welded inseparably." Think

> Like all sin, sexual sin is forgivable. But unlike some other sins, it's also a sin against yourself.

of it this way: the more people to whom you attach your Post-it note, the less staying power a sexual relationship will have.

As the writer of the book of Proverbs put it, you can't walk barefoot on hot coals and not get blisters on your feet (6:28 THE MESSAGE). What happens in Vegas doesn't stay in Vegas; our money stays there, but our experiences come home with us.

And none of us can go back in time and undo what we have done, unsee what we have seen, and not be who we have become over time.

I'm not trying to make you feel bad about your past. Instead, I want to fight for your future. In a later chapter, I'll talk about the power of God to deal with the scars you already have. But for the moment, I have two prayers: First, that you understand you have the power right now to prevent scar tissue down the road. And second, that if people from Discovery Channel or the Tour de France are reading this, they would please space things out in the future. Because Le Shark Week is still haunting my dreams.

CHAPTER 4

Flying Blind

The president's son had seconds to live. He was in the cockpit of a plane he had owned for three months. With a net worth between thirty and one hundred million dollars, he could afford to pay a hundred pilots to fly him, but he liked being at the controls.

The night was dark, and he was in a hurry to get to Martha's Vineyard. He wasn't instrument rated, and conditions were at the outer edge of what he was technically competent to take off in. Choosing to fly that night cost him his life and those of his wife and sister-in-law. On the descent a haze appeared on the horizon, making it impossible to perceive heaven from earth amid the black sky and featureless sea. What felt like flying level was rushing him to a watery grave. The Piper Saratoga II airplane plummeted into the Atlantic Ocean traveling at seventy-nine feet per second. The pilot never issued an emergency call.[1]

The deaths were not just tragic; they were unnecessary. When Navy divers found John F. Kennedy Jr's body, it was still buckled into his seat aboard an aircraft with sophisticated instruments to prevent such a thing from happening. He just didn't trust them when it counted.

Even when you are instrument rated, it can be difficult to trust your instruments while flying in certain conditions. Your eyes and the fluid in your ears can play tricks on you. Both changing weather and lack of daylight can hide the horizon. Spatial disorientation can set in, and soon up seems like down, left feels like right, and wrong becomes right. Pilots call it *black hole vertigo*. It is possible to be absolutely, positively, swear-on-a-stack-of-Bibles certain that you need to descend, when in reality you're heading toward the earth at terminal velocity in a graveyard spiral. JFK died after resisting the Secret Service's pleas to keep the bubble top on his convertible on that fateful day in Dallas; his son lost his life because he couldn't trust the instruments.

I am writing these words while sitting in the back of a small plane. My wife, Jennie, and I squeezed into the tiny cabin with a few of our staff members a little over an hour and a half ago. The plane will take us to Billings, Montana, where we will do a television interview about my book *Through the Eyes of a Lion*. It didn't hit me until right now that most people would consider it bad luck to write a chapter that begins with a plane crash while flying in a Cessna. I would call it inspiration, but I genuinely didn't make the connection until now.

We have flown through clouds so thick I couldn't see two feet outside the window. And as I write this, we are passing through turbulence that is making my laptop jump and jostle in my lap like a tiny bull at a rodeo. But I can see the pilot's gauges from where I'm sitting, and I know that his perception of our direction is not as important as what those instruments are telling him.

Because of the weather, there is no visible horizon, and it will soon be dark anyway. But the altimeter and the course deviation, gyro horizon, turn and slip, vertical speed, and airspeed indicators are sure and reliable markers to fly by. That's a good thing, because somewhere below us are vicious mountaintops waiting to obliterate the first airplane stupid enough to fly into them. If we were to stall suddenly, I'm relying on the pilot to pay attention to the warnings and follow the manual, no matter how he feels about the situation.

In the copilot's seat is a man named John Mark. He used to fly F-16s for the air force but now works at the church I pastor. When I asked him to come with me on this trip, I noted that if something happened to the pilot, he would have to get us home. He nodded his head slightly, accepting the responsibility. I asked him if he had ever gotten disoriented during a mission, and he nodded again, this time more vigorously. With a look of disbelief in his eyes, as though he were still in the cockpit of his $165 million plane, he said, "There was one time when I was absolutely, 100-percent positive that I was flying straight and level, but my instruments told me I was banking right with my nose pointed below the horizon. That means I was in a spiraling dive, headed toward the ground at three hundred miles per hour."

"What did you do?" I pressed.

"I trusted my instruments," he responded. "And it's a good thing, too, since I was only three thousand feet above the ground . . ." His voice trailed off. "It wouldn't have been long before I was dead."

Here is some vital intel you desperately need both in and out of the cockpit: following your feelings can lead to disaster. Solomon said as much in the book of Proverbs: "There is a way that seems right to a man, / But its end is the way of death" (14:12).

Blindly following your heart is a really bad idea. The prophet Jeremiah warned that our hearts are "deceitful" and "desperately wicked" (Jeremiah 17:9). As Anakin Skywalker painfully discovered, going with your gut can destroy your life and everything you hold dear.

Following your feelings can lead to disaster.

You might be tempted to reject that idea entirely, thinking of all the good things following your heart has led you to do and experience. *Levi, you are probably thinking, my college major, career choice, love of cats, and decision to do relief work in Rwanda have all come from following my heart.* I totally get that, and I would agree with you on the goodness of every one of those (except the love of cats). That's why I said we must not follow our hearts *blindly* and that following our feelings *can* lead to disaster. It *can* also lead to wonderful things. But knowing the difference is tricky, and that is precisely why we need a higher authority to guide us.

Just as your heart can make you fall in love with the person of your dreams, it can also make you throw your marriage away for a steamy, short-lived affair. Your feelings can tell you to run someone off the road in rage, just as they can tell you to stop and help a stranded motorist change a tire. Remember the Ashley Madison leaks, which exposed the identities of the users of a popular online service that facilitates people looking to cheat on their spouses? I'll bet you every single person whose reputation and character was tarnished felt as if he knew precisely what he was doing when he signed up. Our most noble achievements, and our most tragic mistakes, all come from the same place: the human heart.

The black box is always opened eventually. Your sin will find you out. Sooner or later, what was done in secret will get tweeted from the rooftops.

Are you gloating? Smugly thinking that your sin hasn't been revealed yet? Know this: it doesn't always happen in this life. Nothing is hidden from the sight of him to whom we must all give an account (Hebrews 4:13).

Just as a pilot needs instruments he can trust, you need objective indicators for your soul. Your feelings aren't irrelevant; they just can't rule your life. Monitor them, but don't trust them. Rather, run them through an objective filter, so that even when you *feel* like doing wrong, you can spot the danger and choose to avoid it.

Do you have a course indicator for your soul? A turn-and-slip indicator that keeps your spiritual feet from slipping? God's Word will do just that. David said it's a lamp to our feet and light for our path (Psalm 119:105). Because our feelings are so subjective, we need the Word of God and the Holy Spirit to guide us. The Word of God keeps us from being fooled by the haze of our emotions and prevents us from being ruled by every thought and desire. C. S. Lewis said, "Aim at Heaven and you will get earth 'thrown in': aim at earth and you will get neither."[2] A spiritual gyro horizon indicator calibrates your heart to focus on things above, even when your appetite here below is screaming something else.

WALKING AROUND IN SQUARES

When I get to heaven, I want to pull up on the DVR the moment when Joshua explained to his generals the plan God gave him to conquer the city of Jericho. They must have gone over all kinds of strategies and plans before General Joshua bumped into the Lord, who told him he and his men were going to defeat the impenetrable fortress of the enemy by walking in circles around it while holding the ark of the covenant—for seven days in a row. I'm sure the generals' blank stares said it all when Joshua got back and enthusiastically explained the plan. "No, you haven't heard the best part! God insisted that we're going to blow our trumpets *and* yell really loud!" *We're goners*, they must have thought.

When our oldest daughter, Alivia, was young, she once grew tired of walking around the grocery store with my wife and, out of desperation, said, "Mom, all we are doing is walking around in squares!" It was an astute observation, really, though she got the phrase wrong; due to the grid-like setup of the store, they were indeed making square-shaped laps, and she had grown tired of all the right angles. Alivia would have sympathized with the Israelites, because no matter what shape their laps made or how loudly they yelled, there was no reason for the Israelites to think those actions would cause walls to fall flat.

Why was Joshua okay with this plan? He knew what we need to know: the specific action was irrelevant; it was the source of the instruction that mattered. It wouldn't have bothered him if God had said, "Wear mime face paint and juggle." God doesn't call us to understand; he wants us to obey. Joshua was the sort of dude whose response to whatever God asked for was, "I can do that." And that's how he changed the world.

It seemed like a crazy plan all right—until it worked. My favorite detail about the story is that the Israelites had no way to know whether the plan was working. They had to get up every day, make a lap around the city, and then go home. On the seventh day, they circled it seven times, just as God had told them to do. Then—and only then—the walls came tumbling down. Did you catch that? Deliverance came only when there had been complete obedience. The walls didn't fall incrementally, a little bit each day; neither did they slowly but surely start to get sketchy as bricks started popping out a la an enormous game of Jenga. There was no way to know what would happen until they had already done something that seemed stupid fourteen times. I would have been so frustrated, because one of the great motivators in any undertaking is seeing how far you've come. The mile markers along the way fuel your forward progress. Any good leader knows this.

"We've come this far! Let's finish it. We can do this. Don't stop now!" is a great speech to fire up a team. This attitude has the same effect spiritually. If God calls you to be kinder or more of a blessing to others, it can be hard at first. But as you obey, you experience little payoffs along the way. The first time someone does something that would normally bring out your inner Hulk, but instead you take a breath and try to show Christ's love, you'll be like, "Wow. That felt good. I want to do that again."

Joshua's undertaking took guts because it provided none of those incremental and tangible demonstrations of progress. If the Israelites had gotten to the end of the seven days and the plan hadn't worked, they would have wasted all that time when they could have been trying something intelligent—like building a siege ramp or tunneling under the walls.

I think it is often this way when God calls us. He tells us to do something that doesn't have any observable benchmarks until the end, and it seems like we're walking in circles or rectangles instead of making headway. Progress isn't always visible.

A woman in our church, who is one of the sweetest and most enthusiastic people I know, posted on Instagram that it wasn't until a friend invited her four times to come to our church that she finally decided to go. The first and second and third time she said, "No way." The fourth time she caved, and since then, God has healed her broken marriage and changed her life forever. Who she is today isn't even close to who she once was. What if the person who invited her gave up and bailed out after strike three?

I can't help but stop and wonder if you might be right there—at the edge of victory. Are you tempted to lose heart and throw in the towel because something you were sure was God's will doesn't seem to be working?

You are trying to be a godly parent, but the kids don't seem to hear anything you tell them.

You are trying to share your faith with a friend, but he or she isn't showing any signs of listening.

You are trying to be a godly, loving wife, but your husband's heart is just as hard toward God as ever.

Please don't give up. The breakthrough you are longing for might come without any indication along the way that what you are doing is working.

Take heart. Trust your instruments. You might be closer to landing than you know.

When my daughter Lenya, who is now in heaven, was three, we were "walking around in squares" at the grocery store when, out of the corner of my eye, I saw her put something down her shirt. I played it cool. I walked over, leaned down, and asked her if she had taken anything.

> The breakthrough you are longing for might come without any indication along the way that what you are doing is working.

"No," she replied immediately, with a confidence that could dupe a polygraph machine.

I was surprised by her Academy Award performance, but I was not deterred. Pointing to her stomach, I asked, "Then what is that lump on your shirt?"

Again she played it off. "Nothing."

"Lenya, take out what I saw you put down your shirt," I instructed her.

Sulking that her cover was blown, she pulled out a tube of Chap Stick. But she hadn't picked it up to soothe dry lips; it was a snack. At that stage of her life, she liked to eat Chap Stick. Jennie would often discover one in her purse with a few mouse-like nibbles, if the flavor was to Lenya's liking.

Right there in the grocery store, Lenya and I had a great conversation about theft, prison, and what would come of a life of crime. Fortunately she was receptive to my pep talk and made the wise choice to return the Chap Stick to the shelf.

Like Lenya, Achan had sticky fingers. Achan was there when the walls came tumbling down. He witnessed an undeniable demonstration of what happens when God's people obey his instructions, despite how counterintuitive they seem at the time. He heard Joshua's rules of engagement, delivered right before the walls fell:

1. Rahab the harlot and any family members in her house, which was marked by a scarlet rope hanging in the window, were not to be harmed. This Canaanite woman, a citizen of Jericho, was in fact a double agent who had risked her life aiding and abetting Israelite spies. Incidentally, she would go on to become the great-great-great . . . (I'll spare you the twenty-four more *greats*) grandmother of Jesus. #NBD

2. In the aftermath of the battle, all money or treasure found in the rubble was to be given immediately to God's treasury, or else a crazy Pirates of the

Caribbean–type curse would be unleashed: "By all means abstain from the accursed things, lest you become accursed when you take of the accursed things, and make the camp of Israel a curse, and trouble it" (Joshua 6:18).

Those were the two rules: Rahab was not to be harmed, and God had dibs on all the spoil. If you didn't expect to hear instructions about rescuing a prostitute and putting all the money from the city in the offering plate, please remember they followed a battle fought by making laps and yelling. This plan had left "making sense" territory a long time ago.

The walls surrounding Jericho fell. Rahab was safely evacuated, and the treasure was collected and deposited. Everything went according to plan. Except one person— Achan—disobeyed. No one knew but his family—and God. He would have gotten away with it, too, except that when he stole the treasure from the rubble of Jericho, he triggered the curse. As a result, Israel lost the next battle they fought; thirty-six men died because of what he had done (Joshua 7:5, 11–12). So, yeah, it was sort of a big problem.

Brought before Joshua to confess, Achan admitted what had happened: "When I saw among the spoils a beautiful Babylonian garment, two hundred shekels of silver, and a wedge of gold weighing fifty shekels, I coveted them and took them. And there they are, hidden in the earth in the midst of my tent, with the silver under it" (v. 21).

Imagine the scene of Achan's crime. Dust and smoke filled the air as the cleanup crew made their way through the debris of the ruins of Jericho. Achan discovered an inner chamber, with a chest hidden behind a Mesopotamian blanket. He called for his friends, but they had already crossed this house off their list. He realized he was by himself—the last person in the city.

He bludgeoned the lock with a rock. Beads of perspiration appeared on his grimy forehead. His heart galloped as he lifted the lid.

A big wedge of gold shone in the torchlight. He took in the sight of the bag of silver coins and the gorgeous tunic, the equivalent of an Armani tuxedo.

Achan knew he was supposed to bring the items to the tabernacle. These belonged to God. But something inside him stiffened. What did God want with a robe anyway? Butterflies whipped tornadoes in his stomach as he looked to his left, then to his right—and knowing full well it was wrong, he swiped the treasure.

I can't help but ask a couple of questions. How did he manage to get the treasure out of there? Did he make multiple trips? Did he pull a Lenya and put stuff under his shirt?

I picture him coming out of the house looking like he's in his third trimester and telling his friends, all squirrelly, "I gotta go use the restroom"—like *Jurassic Park*'s Dennis Nedry smuggling dinosaur embryos in a can of shaving cream.

"Achan, are you okay? You look different," his friends probed.

"Well, I guess I have put on a little weight," he fibbed. "That manna, whoa—not exactly low carb, if you know what I mean. It might have come from heaven, but it's been murder on my figure . . ."

Somehow he smuggled the goods out undetected. (And

unlike what happened to Nedry, no dinosaurs spit venom in Achan's face after he got his Jeep stuck in the mud.) Now what? He couldn't exactly wear the robe to dinner. He couldn't sell it on BCBay or Abraham's List. What was his plan? He was born in the wilderness; there were no malls. There was no good explanation for how he would have come by this stuff. In other words, he wouldn't be able to enjoy what he took after those first few moments when his desires got the best of him.

But he wasn't thinking about that in the moment.

He certainly wasn't thinking about the fact that his disobedience would cause the deaths of thirty-six of his brothers-in-arms, or the fact that his theft would end up costing him and his entire family their lives when they were executed for his crime.

Achan experienced spiritual disorientation. Trapped in a cloud of his own desires, he lost the ability to tell up from down. Alarms must have gone off on the dashboard inside his heart, but he didn't follow the manual; instead he overrode the alarms, did what seemed right to him in the moment, and then buried the proof of his disobedience.

We, too, bury our sins in the dirt. And we desperately hope that what we bury no one will ever dig up. But like Abel's blood of long ago, the sins we hide beneath handfuls of earth cry to the Lord from the ground. We hope to smother our pasts with shovelfuls of soil, but they relentlessly crawl from their shallow graves, like Leonardo DiCaprio in *The Revenant*. Our dark deeds claw toward us, as unstoppable as a man possessed by revenge, bound and determined to harm the future we desperately want to hide from them.

FATHER KNOWS BEST

When you hear God telling you not to have sex outside of marriage, it's easy to misunderstand his motives and feel like he's a killjoy. Achan wasn't the last person in history to think that God doesn't want them to have any booty. It's easy to be suspicious of God and think we need to look out for ourselves.

We live in a culture that is suffering the consequences of not trusting God's plan for sex. Instead, we've loaded up our boxes with all the Babylonian garments and silver and gold we can get our hands on. We haven't realized that when we take what God has told us not to touch, it can prevent him from giving us what he wants us to have.

> We live in a culture that is suffering the consequences of not trusting God's plan for sex.

God isn't saying "not *ever*." He's just saying "not *now*, not *yet*."

God doesn't want you to settle for hidden, rushed, dirty, stolen intimacy. He has something so much better for you.

He wants your honeymoon to be a joy you couldn't imagine, not just business as usual.

He doesn't want your marriage bed to be haunted by pictures and previous partners.

He wants you to enjoy sex to the fullest.

I think when Achan heard God say no, he heard "not

ever." But what God meant was "not now." God said "not now" to the booty at Jericho, knowing Achan could have a much greater treasure to enjoy at Ai and beyond. But Achan was shortsighted; he didn't think of the future, and he didn't trust God. He thought he had to look out for himself, and so he settled for hastily grabbed loot that he hid in the dirt under his tent and couldn't even enjoy. In the end his family was destroyed by his actions.

If I could go back in time and talk to Achan, I would want to tell him about Joshua 8. I would tell him that just before the Israelites invaded the city of Ai, God gave Joshua a pre-mission briefing with only one rule: "You shall do to Ai and its king as you did to Jericho and its king. Only its spoil and its cattle you shall take as booty for *yourselves*" (v. 2, emphasis added). I would explain that this rule would be in effect at every subsequent battle. God did not desire to take something from the Israelites but to give something to them.

But Achan didn't get to see this, because he and his family were stoned and buried under a pile of rocks in the Valley of Achor. He didn't get to see what was in chapter 8 because he died in chapter 7. He ended up under the ground because of what he hid in the ground.

It's tragically, bitterly ironic.

God's rules are there for a reason—not to kill your joy but to enhance it. He has so much more in store for you than you could ever know. But to get there, you must relinquish your desire to navigate on your own, lest you lose your way. When you put your trust in the instruments God has given you, you set yourself up to soar.

CHAPTER 5

Strength and Honor

The woman who designed the Nike swoosh was paid only thirty-five dollars for her work.[1] For a company that is now worth billions, I'd say she got far less for that little checkmark logo than it was worth. At the time it was just a doodle, a little emblem to adorn the running shoes that Bill Bowerman, legendary track coach and cofounder of Nike, was making in his wife's waffle-iron. When the designer sold the swoosh for so little, she could never have known that in time it would be one of the most recognizable symbols in the entire world. To be fair Nike's founders didn't know either, and they could barely afford to pay her what they did; they started on a shoestring budget and almost went under many times on the road to greatness. But keep that fact in mind: thirty-five bucks in exchange for the *Nike logo*.

Achan and Esau both show us how easy it is to make a bad deal in the moment. Satan wants to inflame you with passion so you sell yourself short—for pennies on the billions. He will try to trick you into forfeiting what he could never be able to take without your consent. Please realize that where your birthright and your calling are concerned, you are more dangerous to yourself than the devil is. The temptations of Christ show this clearly. The devil could only tell Jesus to jump off the roof of the temple; he couldn't actually push him. Satan is a defeated foe. When Jesus has your back, the devil has no more power over you than you choose to concede to him. He whispers into your ear but can't make you do anything.

In the time it takes to swipe the screen of a tablet, steam up the windows of a parked car, or ruffle the sheets of a hotel room bed, you can give up much in exchange for so little. What kind of deal is it to get everything you want but lose yourself (Mark 8:36)? I've already described how having sex with someone can scar your heart. By getting into the habit of experiencing sex apart from the context it was designed to be experienced in, I worry you are moving slowly toward a future that you won't like when you get there. Horace Mann said that habits are like cables built of tiny wires braided together: "We weave a thread for it each day and it becomes so strong that we cannot break it."[2]

I have experienced the power of habit firsthand—for both good and evil. I told you briefly about the scar pornography gave me. It created a habit that led to a secret porn addiction that smoldered for years. It clouded how I looked at the young women in my life and in the world in a way I didn't like but felt powerless to change. Even now, if I let my eyes wander or my thoughts roam freely, the enemy is quick to use against me all the ammo I gave him in my adolescence. It has not been easy breaking free from the chains of immorality, but because the weapons of our warfare are mighty (2 Corinthians 10:4), these strong-holds can be torn down. (In chapter 7, I will talk specifically about one of the most important things you can do to fight these temptations.)

Don't misunderstand me: I'm not preaching legalism, as though your standing before God is dependent on your actions. Salvation is a nonstop flight, and Jesus paid your whole way. We don't earn our standing before God the way a prisoner gets access to early parole; it isn't through good behavior that we become pleasing to God. Whom the Son sets free is free indeed (John 8:36). You look no different to God the Father when you are crushing life as when you are being crushed by it. When he sees you, all he sees is Jesus. In your walk with God, you might feel as if you have a case of the Mondays, but on heaven's calendar, it's always Good Friday! Salvation is a gift; you can't lose through bad behavior what you didn't deserve in the first place.

The forgiveness we have been given is so powerful and all-inclusive (it even reaches to sins we haven't committed yet) that we are free to make a mess of our lives. That's why Galatians, a book wholly devoted to breaking the chains of legalism, includes a warning about the fact that our sin natures could deceive us into making unwise decisions (Galatians 5:13). Here's the sober-ing truth: what you do with your liberty can put you back in captivity. If you believe in Jesus, then you are going to

> Salvation is a nonstop flight, and Jesus paid your whole way.

heaven when you leave this earth no matter what, but how much of heaven you experience on this earth, and how much treasure you have waiting for you on that distant shore, has everything to do with what you do now. It's possible to have a saved soul but a wasted life—to have been given everything and to have done nothing with it.

The devil plays dirty. He is not afraid of cheap shots, and he loves hitting below the belt. Sex is certainly not the only effective trick up his sleeve. As far as I can tell, it's one of his top three lures—along with pride and money—and as the old fishing proverb goes, you don't switch your bait when the fish are biting.

Satan wants your story to be a tale of what could have been. He wants all your potential to remain untapped and to be buried with you when you die. Next time you find yourself in a graveyard, imagine how many businesses, songs, inventions, churches, and poems are six feet under because they weren't created before the potential creator's life ended. Open your eyes! If the devil can't take you to hell, he will try to keep you from living for heaven.

THE POWER OF AN APPRAISAL

Think about that woman who gave up the swoosh logo for thirty-five dollars. How do you think she felt seeing her logo on shoes the world over, considering her payday for the project wouldn't even buy her one pair? You don't have to shed too many tears for her, though; a few years later, the company's leadership looked her up and gave her stock in

Nike. An honest appraisal of her contribution led the founders to give her part ownership in the company. The swoosh is as much an element of Nike's iconic status as their "Just do it" slogan. It's part of the package. Their assessment of the part she played made them want to go back in time and redefine the worth of her work. It's a beautiful gesture, because they didn't have to do it.

Generally speaking, I have a love-hate relationship with the appraisal process. It's time-consuming, it's expensive, and it often feels like a racket. Yet once the process is done, there is undeniable power in having a declared value for a piece of property. It answers the question of worth and gives you leverage when approaching banks for a loan or when setting a selling price.

In the same way, it is vital that you are clear about the worth of your soul. The failure to understand your identity will inevitably lead to feelings of insecurity and inferiority. You will start to feel sorry for yourself, and you'll want to change but not really believe change is possible or that you deserve it—and then the enemy can rip you off.

Every morning you should look in the mirror and declare, "I am chosen, loved, called, and equipped." *I don't know, Levi, I don't feel that special.* Excuse me? You are a child of the King, filled with the Holy Spirit that raised Christ from the dead, able to do all things through Him who gives you strength, and as bold as a lion!

You might not have a million followers on Instagram, but you are adored by

> I am chosen, loved, called, and equipped.

God. He knit you together in your mother's womb and has had plans for your life since before you were born (Psalm 139:13, 16). Though you sinned and separated yourself from God, he chose to adopt you as his own.

The idea that we're adopted by God is particularly meaningful. The personality of a child you birth is a mystery; there is no way to know what he or she will be like. You love that baby boy or girl without knowing anything about him or her. But adopting an older child is choosing to bring someone into your life already knowing who he or she is.

God chose you. You weren't a white elephant gift. He wasn't duped by your packaging and disappointed now that he knows you. If you walk out into the world without this knowledge of your worth firmly in mind, you might think your value is vulnerable, which means you can be tricked by the first person to show an interest in you.

GOING BACK TO THE START

It's amazing how messages get mixed up when communication passes through just three or four people. Think of the game of Telephone, which you may have played as a kid: "I like long walks on the beach" can morph into "My cousin is choking on a peach." The further you get from the one who spoke the original words, the more distorted the message may become.

In the same way, God's purpose and plan for relationships and romance has been obscured. We need to go back to the beginning to find out what he had in mind. The two words that should mark our thoughts on sex are *honor* and *strength*.

The word *honor* speaks of worth. If you honor something, you put a high value on it; you esteem it as being precious. To honor something is not to take it lightly or approach it flippantly. Scripture tells us we are supposed to show honor where honor is due (Romans 13:7). No one is higher than the Most High God, who is worthy of all praise, glory, and worship forever (Psalm 145:3; 1 Samuel 2:2; 1 Kings 8:23; Psalm 92:8). Our honor then flows down to all people who were made in God's image. C. S. Lewis reminds us, "There are no *ordinary* people. You have never talked to a mere mortal. Nations, cultures, arts, civilisations—these are mortal, and their life is to ours as the life of a gnat. But it is immortals whom we joke with, work with, marry, snub, and exploit—immortal horrors or everlasting splendours."[3] The honor—or dishonor—we show people we encounter has the potential to help them on their paths to becoming more splendid—or more horrific. When we honor people, we acknowledge that their souls are immortal, that the spark of the divine is within them, and that—whether they run the drive-through at Taco Bell or crisscross the country on a private jet—they matter.

Honor should mark every relationship in our lives. Children are to honor their parents, and parents are to honor their children. Employees should honor their bosses, and bosses are called to honor their employees. We all are to honor those in positions of authority over us: police officers, spiritual leaders, even elected officials. "Honor up, honor down, honor all around," my friend Pastor Kevin Gerald likes to say.

Unfortunately, we live in a day when honor is in short supply. We're experiencing a drought of even basic respect. Everything about our culture is sarcastic, snarky, pessimistic, antiauthority, and rebellious, with an undercurrent of *Who are you to tell me what to do?* I'm reminded of an Old Testament prophecy:

> There is a generation that is pure in its own eyes,
> Yet is not washed from its filthiness.
> There is a generation—oh, how lofty are their eyes!
> And their eyelids are lifted up.
> There is a generation whose teeth are like swords,
> And whose fangs are like knives. (Proverbs 30:12–14)

Sounds a whole lot like the millennial generation I am part of. We were raised on *Beavis and Butthead*, *The Simpsons*, *Salute Your Shorts*, and *Ren and Stimpy*. We are a pretty skeptical bunch, as you can tell from our 140-character-long attention spans and jaded, seen-it-all attitudes.

BRINGING SEXY BACK

The world could do with a great deal more honor, especially when it comes to our love lives. The Bible tells us clearly that marriage and sex are to be honored: "Marriage is honorable among all, and the bed undefiled; but fornicators and adulterers God will judge" (Hebrews 13:4). This verse tells us we need to bring sex back to its proper place—the marriage bed. Sex done right is awesome and should be honored, exalted, and valued. What happens on the honeymoon and in the marriage bed isn't dirty or gross. It isn't defiled or shameful. There's nothing wrong with looking forward to it or being excited about it. The Bible never blushes when it speaks of the joys of sexual pleasure:

> Let your fountain be blessed,
> And rejoice with the wife of your youth.
> As a loving deer and a graceful doe,
> Let her breasts satisfy you at all times;
> And always be enraptured with her love.
> (Proverbs 5:18–19)

The strategy some churches employ to counsel against extramarital sex is lacking. Intentionally or not, they often send the message that sex is dirty, bad, and gross, so we should save it for marriage. But there is nothing wrong with having a sex drive. It's a good thing—a God thing, in fact.

The ultimate proof that God isn't antisex is that sex is his creation. He thought of it and gave it to us to enjoy. Technically, sex was the first gift God gave to Adam—if you don't count the nap. The Bible says that Adam was lonely and had no one to do life with, so God made a deep sleep

The Bible never blushes when it speaks of the joys of sexual pleasure.

fall over him. (Boom! The world's first nap.) And when he woke up, there she was: Eve. He liked what he saw so much that he wrote a poem on the spot: "Bone of my bones / And flesh of my flesh" (Genesis 2:23). Translated from the original Hebrew, it loosely means "Dang, girl!" And then something Drake-esque about how even if Eve had a twin he would still pick her . . .

God was pleased with Adam's reaction. God didn't correct Adam. He wasn't offended. He didn't chide him: "*Adam!* Get your mind out of the gutter!" He brought the guy a naked wife, so I assume he knew what was going to happen next. In fact, dead center in the book of Song of Solomon (basically the Bible's version of sex education), you'll find an invitation, which many commentators attribute to God himself, to enjoy the gift of the marriage bed: "Eat, O friends! / Drink, yes, drink deeply, / O beloved ones!" (5:1).

God wants us to enjoy sex within marriage. He wants it to be incredible and rocking. He knows it feels good. It was designed to be that way! Sex doesn't exist only to bring babies into the world but to bring joy, excitement, fun, and pleasure into our lives.

But God knows that sex is not only pleasurable—it's also powerful. So it came with instructions. The chainsaw you buy at Home Depot can do a lot of good, but it can also chop off your leg! God, too, gave us guidelines, but people think he is a prude and a killjoy. It's ridiculous, really. Do you think Apple is a buzzkill because the instructions tell you not to take your iPhone swimming with you? Are they phone-o-phobic? Of course not! We understand that the rules help us get the most out of our phones. Far from proving he is against it, the fact that God tells us how to do sex the right way shows he cares about it.

SEX ED, GARDEN OF EDEN STYLE

Straight from the manufacturer, here are the guidelines for sex that God gave right after he created it: "Therefore a man shall leave his father and mother and be joined to his wife, and they shall become one flesh" (Genesis 2:24). In the New Testament, Jesus affirmed the verse and followed it up with, "What God has joined together, let not man separate" (Matthew 19:6). Paul referred to this verse when he warned the Corinthians not to treat sex as only physical— because it triggers a union on the inside you can't reverse (1 Corinthians 6:16).

So, to recap: sex is to be enjoyed in a marriage relationship by one man and one woman who have left their parents to start a new life together and are committed to each other for a lifetime.

That's it. Those are the instructions. They are so simple you could tweet them.

As long as sex stays in the marriage bed, go nuts! But recall the warning from Hebrews 13:4: "Fornicators and adulterers God will judge." When sex is taken out of its proper place, it can wreak havoc and unleash judgment on your life. This verse specifically mentions two inappropriate uses of sex: fornication (sex before marriage) and adultery (sex outside of marriage).

There are a whole host of other ways to misuse sex—one man with three women, two men, a woman with an animal, an adult with a child—but rather than listing every possibility of what *not* to do, we need to focus on what we *should* do.

When contained to the fireplace or the stove, fire can heat a home and cook your food. Likewise, sex in the marriage bed can heat up your marriage. But outside the specific environments where they can be controlled, both fire and sex destroy lives and burn homes to the ground.

Scripture uses an all-encompassing "junk drawer" word to describe sex outside the marriage bed: *immorality*. In Greek, the word is *porneia*, and it's the origin of the English word *pornography*. And here is what God has to say about immorality and you: "This is the will of God, your sanctification: that you should abstain from sexual immorality; that each of you should know how to possess his own vessel in sanctification and honor, not in passion of lust, like the Gentiles who do not know God" (1 Thessalonians 4:3–5). It's not having a sex drive that is the problem; rather, it's letting sex drive and doing whatever you feel like.

We turn from God's plans because we think we'll have more fun, but just the opposite is true: sexual experience before marriage doesn't make you better at sex. Studies show that those who don't have a background of pornography or previous partners tend to have a higher level of sexual pleasure in marriage than those who do.[4] Sexually active singles have the most sexual problems, get the least pleasure out of sex, and are more likely to experience depression.[5]

Living together doesn't prepare you for marriage;

instead, it shoots the relationship in the foot. Studies have shown a "cohabitation effect": couples who live together before marriage are more likely to divorce than couples who do not. In contrast, married couples reported the happiest satisfaction with their sex lives. The most sexually satisfied demographic group of them all: married men and women between fifty and fifty-nine.[6] And there's this: studies suggest that married people will have better health and wealth and will probably die happier than singles, with a lower likelihood of strokes, heart disease, and depression. Married people even respond better to stress and heal more quickly.[7]

It seems that the real secret to rocking sex isn't being a player, making booty calls, or scheduling Netflix-and-chill sessions with a different person each weekend. The secret is saving this precious gift for marriage and then making up for lost time.

Honor is the path to your greatest pleasure.

Don't treat yourself like a flimsy Styrofoam cup or a utilitarian diner mug. You are like a piece of fine china: delicate and beautiful.[8] Be careful what you allow to be put inside you and whom you allow to handle you. You are a one-of-a-kind work of art, and the impact you are meant to have on this world extends far beyond your lifetime.

Talking about treating sex with honor is easy, but living it out is a whole 'nother thing. This is where *strength* comes in. It takes strength to rise up in honor. It's not going to happen by accident or by default, and it might even cost you something.

Honoring God's plan for sex isn't easy, but nothing that's truly great ever is. Being broke is easy; saving your money is hard. Being out of shape takes no effort; developing a six-pack takes real work. I have found that, outside of receiving salvation by grace, nothing sweet comes without sweat. Writing a book, launching a successful business, painting a masterpiece, getting an advanced degree, making it in the music industry—these great things all take serious effort. Good things come to those who hustle. We covet the success of others but have no idea what they were willing to go through to get where they did. Biz Stone, cofounder of Twitter, wrote, "Timing, perseverance, and ten years of trying will eventually make you look like an overnight success."[9] No one likes discipline in the moment, but being undisciplined physically, entrepreneurially, financially, or spiritually can cause problems.

You must be willing to fight—for your marriage (now or in the future) and for your calling. For the sons and daughters still unborn who, through the grace of God and your sweat equity, will grow up in a different home environment than you did. You need to fight for the souls of those whom God wants you to reach, but you'll never get the chance to reach them if you sell yourself short. I'm not here to tell you to kiss dating good-bye. I'm here to tell you if you don't fight for honor, then you're kissing the life Jesus died for you to live good-bye.

As pastors Warren Wiersbe and David Wiersbe wrote, "The Christian life is not a playground; it's a battleground."[10] Life and death are hanging in the balance. The devil is not playing checkers but chess: what he is doing over here is so he can do something much worse three moves from now. Don't be a pawn!

Jesus said we need to be as "wise as serpents and harmless as doves" (Matthew 10:16). A dove is harmless, dependent, and a perfect picture of worship. Snakes are aggressive and active, and they have a plan. God wants you to be a *snake-bird*. Confused? Let me explain.

The approaches to God's plans for sex I have heard tend to be either heavily spiritual or all practical. All snake or all bird. But we need both theological and logical, a blend of spiritual and practical. Faith in God leads to actions—it isn't a substitute for actions. Pray to God, yes, but don't be stupid! This is important in all areas of life; for example, don't just pray for a job—apply too! You can't just let go and let God; you have a part to play. It takes strength. Romans 13:14 is a total snakebird verse: "But put on the Lord Jesus Christ" (that's the bird part), "and make no provision for the flesh, to fulfill its lusts" (snake). That is the Bible equivalent of the adage from the Revolutionary War, "Trust God but keep your powder dry!"

The world needs Jesus, and we can't help others if we are so enslaved to sexual sin that we can't see straight. Suit up for battle, pray always, be sober and vigilant, surround yourself with godly people, don't expose yourself to more temptation than would be wise, hide God's Word in your heart, and rely on the power of the Holy Spirit. Be a snake-bird. You were born for this!

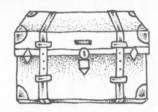

CHAPTER 6

The Things We Carry

I am a chronic overpacker. My life includes a lot of plane trips, so you would think I would be better at it. But because of my frequent-flyer status, I don't have to pay to check bags or fork over extra for overstuffed ones, so there aren't any of the usual incentives to pack light or keep my suitcase under fifty pounds. I can pack whatever I might need, and I don't have to carefully roll items into sushi or play Suitcase Tetris with my clothing. Knowing this has removed inhibitions that are probably better left in place. I am not proud to admit that my wife recently caught me packing five pairs of shoes for a weekend trip. (I like to keep my options open. And I really have a problem with shoes. And, as long as I'm being honest, I didn't have five pairs when I got home—I had six, because I scored a pair of half-price boots on the trip. They were pretty much giving them away.)

Overpacking isn't expensive for me. But the problem is that the suitcase is just plain *heavy*. You have to lug what you load.

Before my daughter Lenya went to heaven, there were six of us—Jennie, me, and our four daughters. Maxed out, our payload would be six large suitcases, six carry-ons, four car seats, and a double stroller. Because Jennie would push the stroller with the two babies, and Liv and Lenya could barely manage their rolling bags, I would be left trying to manage four suitcases and all the car seats. I learned right away to get a Smarte Carte. Best five dollars I ever spent. But even then, the car seats don't ever really stay on top of the suitcases. Once, we were making our way through a car rental facility, trying to find stall #117, when the entire tower fell over, littering suitcases and car seats from Hertz all the way to Alamo.

Everyone who takes a plane brings something on board—purses, laptops, backpacks, Rollaboards. Some go in the overhead compartment; others are stowed at the feet. More checked luggage is stored in the cargo hold. Just as surely as we pack bags for trips, we all bring baggage with us into marriage.

In addition to baggage, passenger planes carry a different kind of box: a black box that records every action the pilot and copilot take. Our lives, too, are equipped with invisible black boxes. Everything we do, from birth to the grave, gets recorded, date-stamped, and logged. Altitude, elevation, transgression, passion, fornication—it all goes in the box.

One day, perhaps far off in the distance, when you decide to settle down and get married, that box will be sitting at the foot of your bed. Whomever you marry will have a box of his or her own too. You won't be able to see the boxes, because the most important parts of a person are invisible. But make no mistake: the contents of those boxes will have an undeniable presence and impact on your home. Galatians 6:5 makes it clear that "every man must 'shoulder his own pack'" (PHILLIPS).

Imagine that you're working out at the gym when a superhot person smiles at you from another machine. They come on to you, you exchange numbers, and you start texting. You meet for dinner, one thing leads to another, and you wake up in their apartment. That experience goes in the box. So does that trip to Mardi Gras, that spring break (woo-hoo!) in Cancun, every frat party, every romance novel, every pornographic website, and every time you hit it and quit it after firing up Tinder, OkCupid, or whatever app facilitated a fast and easy hookup. It all goes in the box.

> The most important parts of a person are invisible.

You might be thinking, *Hold on, Levi, God can forgive! I can do what I want now and then later straighten up. I'll ask for forgiveness down the road, and it will all be fine.* Of course God can forgive you—but he'd much rather be blessing you and using you. Plus, consequences and forgiveness are two different things.

God can forgive you even if you murder someone, but that doesn't mean you should do it. Willfully sinning with the plan of asking for forgiveness later is putting God to the test. It's jumping off a relational cliff and thinking

> Of course God can forgive you—but he'd much rather be blessing you and using you.

you will pull the ripcord later. It's just what the devil wants. He hopes he can deceive you into living a life that is all but impossible for God to bless. He wants your future to be so wracked by bad decisions and foolish choices that you can't enjoy what Jesus died for you to have.

Of those you know who have been divorced, is it possible that their marriages ended because of things they did before they ever met each other? It could be that things they hoped would stay behind them—habits, debt, relationships, decisions—refused to stay buried. Perhaps their failed marriage could have been prevented had they been more aware of the boxes they were packing.

In the military, each soldier is assigned a chest called a footlocker. That name fits the analogy I'm making here because it describes what having a boxful of bad decisions will do: lock up your feet and cause you to stumble. Heed the warning of Proverbs 5:22: "The shadow of your sin will overtake you; / you'll find yourself stumbling all over yourself in the dark" (THE MESSAGE).

The consequences of poor choices don't go away when you tie the knot. Pastor Andy Stanley said, "The only thing that changes at a wedding is a last name. Everything else remains the same, including your bad relational habits and your lack of self-control."[1] When we pick someone to marry we often worry about the wrong things—biceps, breasts, bank account—when perhaps we should be asking how much junk is in their trunk.

There is a great line in one of the Avengers movies. Hulk asks Vision if he is a monster, and Vision replies, "Maybe I am a monster. I don't think I'd know if I were one."

The line stuck with me. Would *I* know if I were a monster? We see what we want to see.

That's the troubling thing about self-deception. It's easy to end up like Bruce Willis's character in *The Sixth Sense*: completely unaware of what is really going on. Every one of us has our own blind spots. It's possible to tell a lie so long you believe it. This is why the Bible warns about the deceitfulness of sin. It is very tricky and can turn you into a monster without your realizing it is happening.

My prayer is that you will have less to carry down the road because of how you live today. Because your present will one day be your past, you can protect your future by living carefully right now. One decision at a time, and quicker than you realize, the box that is your life can become an unwieldy monster, or it can remain free from the heartache of sin that brings bondage and remorse. Washing your hands regularly, getting plenty of sleep, and staying hydrated to avoid getting sick is better than taking all the NyQuil and Theraflu in the world after you've gotten sick. You don't have to treat symptoms from an infection you never got in the first place.

I write on behalf of "Future You," who wants me to let "Today You" know you would rather not be saddled with debt from purchases you haven't made. Future You says you don't want to have the sticky residue of all the sexual partners you haven't yet slept with on the inside of your soul. Future You wants me to let you know it's not cool being haunted by the ghosts of pornography you haven't looked at yet. There are divorces you don't have to go through, STDs you never need to contract, strongholds you needn't let the enemy build in your heart, pleasure and power that you aren't required to forfeit. (Future You also wants me to tell you that having a little extra in the savings account is better than buying things you will end up throwing out or giving away. And you should start flossing, and try to take better care of your skin.) Anything you don't put in your box now, you won't have to carry in the future.

DOWN BUT NOT OUT

But, Levi, you are thinking, *that's all well and good for those sweet, innocent young people who haven't yet racked up any consequences. Don't get me wrong: I am glad you have a message for them—but I have some miles on my tires and some junk in my trunk.*

I get it. You're happy my message will hit hearts that aren't yet calcified with the residue and detritus from relationship wreck after relationship wreck, yet you wish you had read this book ten or twenty years ago.

I'm right there with you. I'm trying to provide for others what I wish I had been told in middle school.

If that's what you're thinking, I'm sure it has been painful to read much of this book, and you are probably feeling pretty discouraged about now. *Let's see: I've forfeited my birthright, I'm a shark covered in scars, I've stolen Babylonian garments that are probably going to get me killed, and I've got to lug around a box filled with all my mistakes for the rest of my life. Thanks for the encouragement!*

Recently, I spoke on the message of this book at my

friend Jack Graham's church in Dallas, and a woman came up to me afterward with tears in her eyes. She appeared to be in her late sixties, maybe early seventies. She grabbed my hand and said something I will never forget: "If I had heard this message fifty years ago, it would have saved me fifty years of regret."

I certainly didn't write this book just for people who have already chosen to swipe right and stick to God's plan for sex and dating. If so, I wouldn't be allowed to read it. I need an emotional Smarte Carte for all the baggage I wish I hadn't packed! The good news for her and for you and for me is that there is still hope. Even if your mistakes seem final and have hurt those closest to you, like Achan's choices did, God can make the valley of Achor (the place where hope was buried) turn into a door of hope (Hosea 2:15).

Listen to me very carefully: *It's not too late.* You're not too far gone. Your greatest days can come after your biggest failures. God specializes in redemption stories. Jesus turned water into wine, and he can make something new out of you.

He doesn't just create—he can re-create.

He doesn't just forgive—he abundantly pardons.

He can bring beauty out of ashes and light from dark places.

He can make a way where there is no way!

I'm not saying it'll be easy or that every consequence will go away. And no, you can't change the past. But if you

Listen to me very carefully: *It's not too late.*

give God your present, he will begin a new chapter in your story. Just because you can't unreap what you have already sown doesn't mean you can't start sowing something new. I dare you to believe that what feels like a big, fat mess right now can bloom into a powerful message, and that, as in David's fifty-first psalm, even your sin can turn into a song.

Remember Rahab, the woman from Jericho we talked about in chapter 4? She had given safe refuge to two Israelite spies and as a result was promised protection when the city was destroyed. She was told to mark her house by putting a scarlet cord in her window, and all within her house would be saved (Joshua 2:1–21). Do you remember what she did for a living? The Bible tells us she was a harlot. Translation: a prostitute. People paid her to have sex with them.

I don't know how Rahab ended up as a prostitute, though I'd bet that as a little girl it wasn't what she had wanted to be when she grew up. Maybe she was reduced to such a living by the death of her husband and had no other way to take care of her impoverished family. That still happens today, you know: women experience tragedy and feel they have no option besides selling their bodies to pay the bills.

My heart broke as I did a little research to try to get myself into Rahab's head. The average age of entry into prostitution in America is thirteen years old.[2] The National Center for Missing and Exploited Children reports that factors common to youth who have been prostituted include suffering violence in the home, experiencing disrupted family life, being placed in foster care, and running away. As many as 60 percent of runaways end up resorting to prostitution.[3]

People sometimes resort to selling themselves to feed an addiction. I'm sure when they experienced their first highs, they never thought they would resort to prostitution to get their fixes. Sexual abuse can play a role, too: as many as 80 percent of prostitutes were abused sexually at some point.[4] Then there is the growing epidemic of human trafficking—an estimated forty-six million people are trapped in modern-day slavery, and a great deal of them are sexually exploited.[5] Around the world, our country included, young children are sold on auction blocks and put into brothels where they are forced to service up to thirty-five or forty men a day.[6]

So Rahab must have felt trapped in a lifestyle that she no doubt wanted out of. How do I know that? Most do. One study has shown that almost 90 percent of prostitutes want to quit but lack resources to do so.[7]

I'm sure Rahab wanted out with all her heart. I just love that out of the entire city of Jericho, she was the only one who turned to God and was given the promise of salvation and safe passage out of the city. But that's not all. Her background might have made religious people cringe, but God had big plans for her life. He saw not what she was but what she could become.

That's who God is and what he does.

He is a redeemer of broken things.

A mender of what is ripped.

A healer of what is hurt.

There is no one too far gone or too messed up for him to reach.

Rahab went on to marry a man named Salmon, the son

of Judah's military commander (Numbers 2:3; Ruth 4:20). God had a happily-ever-after in mind for her, and her name has a funny way of popping up in the New Testament. In fact, she's mentioned as many times as her contemporary Joshua, the successor of Moses himself!

The author of Hebrews praised her for her faith and pointed to her as an example to follow (Hebrews 11:31). Only two women in all of history are mentioned by name in the "hall of faith" presented in Hebrews 11—Rahab and Sarah.

Then she pops up again in James 2:25, where she is praised for the works her faith produced. James uses only two Old Testament individuals as examples—Abraham, the father of faith, and Rahab, the former harlot. Once again, she is put on a pedestal and held up as an example. Instead of pointing to one of any number of good people who had neat and tidy lives, James chose her.

But her most important appearance comes right at the beginning of the Gospels. If you are familiar with the Bible you probably have stumbled over the long list of names that opens the first chapter of Matthew. If you are just starting out reading the Scriptures, the list can be off-putting. You might wonder, *What the heck is this phone book supposed to mean?* Ancient people identified themselves according to who their ancestors were, not by what they had accomplished themselves. The list of names was the paperwork certifying Jesus was who he said he was; it verifies the messianic line that produced both King David and King Jesus. And in Matthew 1:5 is the most unlikely of individuals: Rahab the harlot!

This is as scandalous and shocking as it is touching.

Some religious people might look down their noses at someone such as Rahab and judge her, thinking to themselves, *What a sinner!* Of course, Jesus would be like, "Seriously? You're talking smack about my grandma?"

Here's a reality check for any modern-day Pharisees: Jesus died on the cross with former prostitute blood flowing in his veins.

Next time you think that you're too messed up for God to use you, remember that. He became one of us so he could make us like him. No matter where you have been or what you have done, Jesus is your family. We would do better to burn our churches to the ground than let them become places where a person like Rahab isn't welcome.

I dare you to believe your best days are still waiting for you.

I thought of Rahab when I received this note from a young girl who ended up in our ministry:

Pastor Levi,

I just wanted to say thank you. Fresh Life Church saved my life. I've been raped, abused, neglected, and anything else you can imagine. Then one of my friends brought me to Skull Church, and I can remember every detail from when I walked down that aisle and gave my life to Jesus Christ. I know that God will be with me wherever I go. Every time I mess up or feel like I'm about to panic, I imagine something you said in church: "I won't give up. Instead I'll get back up, and I'll get back up, and I'll get back up." Since my walk with Jesus Christ, when I made that decision, I have lost so many friends—even my own dad told me how ridiculous I am. God has given me strength I cannot even describe. Sometimes, when I look back, I feel like a completely different person. I am afraid (to do what God is calling me to), but I need to do what you said and "activate my calling."

Thank you so much.

HOPE CHESTS AND GLORY BOXES

While I've been writing this book, I've definitely experienced some tension. On the one hand, I write for my daughters and a whole generation like them who never need to accumulate a whole boxful of consequences. I want them to follow in my wife's footsteps. Jennie is a model of strength and honor. But I also wanted to write for people like me—people who have not always swiped right—but to do so in a way that doesn't cause them to think they should do what they want now and then pull the rip cord and have what God wants later.

> True grace is shocking and seems so comprehensive that it's almost absurd.

Preaching the idea of grace always highlights that tension. It is so powerful, so absolute, and so all-consuming that it seems too good to be true. If it doesn't make you uncomfortable, it probably isn't being accurately portrayed. True grace is shocking and seems so comprehensive that it's almost absurd.

I can't reconcile the tension— and I don't want to. Both of these things are true: it's always better to do things God's way, and no matter what you have done, he can work in your life and wash you clean.

There was a time when just about every family who had a young girl would build her a big box made out of cedar. The box, called a hope chest, was a box for the future, a reminder that the young girl would get married one day. As the girl matured and turned into a young woman, her parents would slowly fill the chest with all the things she would need when she became a wife. "We hope one day God brings this man to you, and so you're going to need these things," they'd say. This was their version of a Target wedding registry: Towels. Dishes. Sheets. Cooking utensils. I'm sure the parents involved their daughters in the process, but I love the idea of a mom or dad shopping at the market and seeing something for their daughter's hope chest. It was a constant reminder that the future was coming, and what was in the box would be of assistance when it was time.

I can hardly type this as I think about someday giving my daughters away, but the day would finally come when the young woman would get married. Back in the day the items for the dowry, the payment the bride's family would give to the groom, went into the chest. This would be the parents' wedding gift to their daughter. The box would be taken into her new home to sit at the foot of the bed, and all of its contents filled the newly married couple's lives. A bride would often place her wedding dress in the chest, and if she had a daughter of her own, she would pass on the chest to her.

It's a very pretty tradition—I love the rugged permanence

of it. In an IKEA world, where most furniture can hardly survive more than a move, there is an appeal to anything that's not so disposable.

To those with empty chests, I implore you: fill them only with things you will want in the future. But allow me to also talk to those who, like me, have accumulated some baggage you wish you hadn't.

When I was researching hope chests on Wikipedia, I read that in some cultures a hope chest is called a glory box.[8] It's not every day that Wikipedia ministers to me so profoundly, but I had a powerful worship experience when I read that. God spoke to my heart so distinctly. If your spiritual hope chest is full of things you wish you could take back, he wants me to tell you how to turn your gory box into a glory box.

You can find in the Bible a model for this kind of redemption. In the story, told first in Exodus 25 and retold in Hebrews 9:4, God commanded the Israelites to make a box and fill it with reminders of the worst things they had ever done. The Bible calls the box an ark, but it was basically a trunk. What came next was full of heartache.

God said, "I want you to take a pot of the food that I gave you when you complained and doubted that I would take care of you; that's going to remind you that you didn't trust me. And then I want you to take the rod of Moses that budded—you remember that? When you rebelled against the leadership I put over you, and I proved to you Moses was my guy by causing flowers to spring out of a stick? Only then did you trust me, but still thousands died on that day, because a hole opened up in the earth and the rebels were swallowed. Remember that day? Not a great day for you. Let's put that in the box as well. Then add that list of laws I gave to Moses. That'll remind you of everything I said your life should be like but hasn't been like" (Hebrews 9:4, author's paraphrase).

The Israelites were going to have to carry this trunk around as a reminder of their biggest failures. There would be no getting away from it.

Fortunately God said, "I want you to cover the ark in gold and make two angels to spread their wings over the top of it. And I want you to put it in a tent dubbed the tabernacle, the holiest spot on earth" (Exodus 25:18; 26:33, author's paraphrase).

And one day each year, God would allow the high priest to enter into the Holy of Holies—the room where the ark was kept—with the blood of bulls and goats that had just been ritually slaughtered. Hebrews 10:11–14 explains that this offering was essentially the blueprint for what really happened when Jesus died on the cross:

> And every priest stands ministering daily and offering repeatedly the same sacrifices, which can never take away sins. But this Man, after He had offered one sacrifice for sins forever, sat down at the right hand of God, from that time waiting till His enemies are made His footstool. For by one offering He has perfected forever those who are being sanctified.

As the ultimate High Priest, Jesus entered the throne room of heaven with his own blood. After making a payment for our transgressions, he sat down on top of our failures. With the angels over him crying, "Holy, holy, holy," he waits for us to come boldly to his throne to obtain mercy and help in time of need. When you have the blood of Jesus on top of your story, it puts an *L* in the gory and releases God's glory. The gory box becomes the glory box. Yes, it would have been better never to have made the mistakes in the first place, but Jesus is bigger than our failures, and his love covers all our sins.

When the enemy wants to condemn you, his goal is to dig up your box and rub your nose in sins that have been forgiven. But if you are under the blood of Jesus, the only way he can do that is by dethroning Jesus himself—which is impossible. Psalm 29:10 says that God "sat enthroned at the Flood" and "sits as King forever."

No matter what you've done, if you remember to keep the blood of Jesus on top of you, God can't even see your sin because you are hidden in your Savior. When you have that message locked in your heart, you are unstoppable. Nothing can separate you from the love of God (Romans 8:38–39).

I don't care what kind of a monster you may have become. Jesus can and will work in your life. God is not afraid of what's behind you. Yesterday is over, and today a new day is dawning in your life. He wants to use you in ways you wouldn't believe even if he told you.

The whole world, including some Christians, might judge you for what you've done. But not Jesus. It doesn't matter if the whole world looks at you and sees a scarlet *A* on your chest; Jesus' blood puts a scarlet cord in your window—and, as it did Rahab, redemption awaits you.

CHAPTER 7

Red Bull at Bedtime

All I knew about Utica, New York, was that a branch of the Dunder Mifflin paper company almost lost its copy machine to the Scranton branch when Michael Scott, Dwight Schrute, and a very reluctant Jim Halpert tried to steal it in retribution for Karen Filippelli's attempt to recruit Stanley Hudson for her sales team.[1] It is a little bit sad to me that I can find myself in a real city with an actual history dating back to colonial times, yet the only thing I know about it (without going to Google) involves three actors in a PT Cruiser wearing fake mustaches. But *The Office* is my go-to show when traveling. If I feel like I am losing my mind on an airplane, I can bust it out and am able to get through the flight.

My brother-in-law and I were on our way to a conference in Utica, so we flew into Syracuse, where we planned to spend the night. I almost always bring someone with me on preaching trips because it's helpful to have someone around to lend a hand. And Brandon has precisely one hand to lend: he was born with just one. The lack of a second hand has never stopped him from doing anything. He plays guitar, drums, and piano; he takes things apart and fixes them; and recently he built a dining room table. In every possible sense of the word he is more handy than I will ever be.

We got to the hotel close to midnight and made plans for the next day. We had to be at the conference early, and Utica was an hour away, so we decided we would hit the gym first thing in the morning and then leave for the conference. I asked the front desk manager, who had overheard our discussion of wake-up times, when the café in the lobby opened. To my utter disappointment he informed us, "Not that early." Early wake-ups go down easier with coffee.

In our hotel room we found an enormous gift basket that the church sponsoring the conference had delivered as a thank-you gift—and lo and behold, it contained a Red Bull! I was relieved to know that I would be able to get some caffeine into my jet-lagged body after all.

I set out my gym clothes by the door (because it's a total admission of failure to put them away instead of putting them on); then I placed the Red Bull on the dresser. As is my custom, I FaceTimed Jennie and the girls to say good night. We talked about how I was in New York, and they were in Montana, and Lenya is in heaven—we are totally spread out right now, but we will all be reunited one day. Not too long after that, I drifted off to sleep. I might have watched an episode of *The Office* first.

My eyes shot open, burning and tired. Morning already. I was jittery and agitated, as I often am when I have an early wake-up call coming. I had overslept!

I couldn't believe I hadn't heard the phone call. I tore off the covers and headed to the bathroom, where I splashed water on my face. I slowly put on my workout clothes and tried to shake the sleepiness off. I cracked open the Red Bull and gulped it down.

Just then I noticed the alarm clock on the bedside table. Squinting my eyes, I realized it said 3:04 a.m. The numbers didn't make sense to me. I tried to remember what time I was supposed to be awake and hazily realized that there was a very good reason I hadn't heard the wake-up call—it wasn't supposed to come for a few more hours. Sheepishly I looked down at the now empty Red Bull in my hand and thought, *What have I done?*

I kicked off my Nikes, lay back down in bed, and thought of the two messages I would need to preach later that day. I really needed some sleep before that happened.

I closed my eyes but could already feel the caffeine quickening my pulse. Needless to say, no amount of counting sheep would knock me out after that. I tossed and turned like an insomniac, finally dozing off just in time for the real wake-up call. I had to get up for real just as the effects of the energy drink were leaving my system. I felt like I had been run over by a train—and now I had no pick-me-up to drink. I had been betrayed by what I had put into my body.

GARBAGE IN, GARBAGE OUT

I wonder if trying to fall asleep having just chugged a can full of a drink specifically designed to "give you wings" isn't an appropriate and unfortunate picture of what so often sets us back in our attempts to live for God. I am sure you have the best of intentions. You want to do what is right and have healthy relationships. If you aren't making forward progress, it is probably not for lack of trying. Maybe you already spend quiet time with God, attend a small-group Bible study, and serve at your church on a volunteer team.

Perhaps the problem isn't what you aren't doing, but what you are consuming. Could the solution be so simple? I know this: you will have a much better night's sleep without the late-night energy drink.

Your spiritual Red Bull might be the magazines you read, the movies you watch, or the company you keep. It might even be the things you think about; you can't live right if you don't think right. You might not be looking at literal pornography; but steamy romance novels, *Maxim*, the *Sports Illustrated* Swimsuit Issue, anything on late-night Cinemax, and even unchecked roaming of Instagram are the enemies of your soul. There's nothing soft about any kind of porn. Trying to live a life that is pleasing to the Lord while your mind is full of all sorts of supersexual images and ideas is like holding a donut in one hand and a kale smoothie in the other and wondering why you aren't losing weight. In both cases, you're betrayed by what you're putting into your body.

The problem we must face head-on is that, in a very real way, what you allow in your soul could be what short-circuits your spiritual growth and keeps you in a state of arrested development. Proverbs 23:7 points out that a man is what he "thinks in his heart." That means that if you don't filter your thoughts, your soul will become as toxic as the fish aquarium in *Finding Nemo*. You'll be easy pickings for the enemy, who prowls about like a roaring lion, waiting to peel your skin from your bones (1 Peter 5:8). Yikes!

WHY EVEN PICTURES ARE A PROBLEM

All sexual activity—even looking at pornography—alters the makeup of who you are. Some people feel looking at the menu is fine, as long as they don't order; but Jesus equated looking at another person lustfully with committing spiritual adultery (Matthew 5:28). Translation: pornography messes with you.

The Bible isn't the only place saying this, either. Studies have found that "regular porn users are more likely to report depression and poor physical health than nonusers are."[2] Why? If sex is only a biological urge, how on earth does looking at naked pictures eventually make you sick and depressed? Maybe the reason goes much deeper than you think.

A headline on CNN's website caught my eye: "The Demise of Guys."[3] The article was co-written by a psychologist named Dr. Philip Zimbardo, a professor emeritus at Stanford University whose research sounds the alarm about what pornography and video games are doing to young men today. According to his research, the young men who play video games and use porn the most "are being digitally rewired in a totally new way that demands constant stimulation," causing a condition he calls "arousal addiction." He explained that while traditional addictions cause a person to crave more of the same substance (more cocaine, more alcohol), people addicted to porn and video games need more of something different: games that are increasingly more intense or porn that is increasingly darker. This obsession causes many to sacrifice their schoolwork and relationships in the pursuit of their need for a buzz.

Even actor Russell Brand—who, in a 2012 interview with Conan O'Brien, spoke against condom laws for porn actors because condoms would "take the fun out of it"[4] and in 2006 boasted that it wasn't uncommon for him to have sex with five girls a day[5]—has used his platform to speak up about the dangers of porn. Seemingly out of nowhere, Brand uploaded a video to YouTube that warns how unhealthy porn is. Because of pornography, he claimed, "Our attitudes toward sex have become warped and perverted." He admitted, "I think my own relationship with pornography is kind of the hub of my feelings of inner conflict and doubt."[6]

Pornography has become such a problem that boys as young as twelve are sent to live-in porn detox camps—some lasting as long as nine months—to kick the porn habit. One teenager enrolled at one such organization said he had been watching pornography for up to nine hours a day on his Nintendo DS. He had been sleeping only two hours a night, and he was desperate to quit but didn't know how. Another organization's director said, "It's killing us. When a young man or woman gets ahold of this stuff and they start chasing this dopamine high, they stop going to school, their relationships are sabotaged, their intimacy levels drop—everything just becomes skewed."[7]

Over time, exposure to pornography makes you incapable of being sexually turned on without it. An April 2016 cover story in *Time* magazine explained how many young men (and women, too) in America believe growing up with their brains marinated in porn since adolescence has sabotaged their sexual response and wiped out their ability to have actual intercourse with a person right in front of them.[8] Porn doesn't make sex better; it makes it *worse*. You can't spend hundreds of hours looking at thousands of naked, airbrushed, artificial, young bodies and then expect to be satisfied with one real, imperfect, aging person when you get married.

> Porn doesn't make sex better; it makes it *worse*.

If you are hooked on pornography when you're single, you will bring your addiction into your marriage, and it will rot your relationship from the inside out.

The same is true if you are reading pornography. Romance novels are a billion-dollar-a-year industry,[9] and erotic books have been described by book analysts as cannibalizing the genre.[10] We live in a world that sees things in "fifty shades of gray," but God wants us to see the difference between black and white.

I've heard people say it takes only fifteen minutes to look at a *Playboy* but fifteen years to forget what you saw. Well, it has been more than twenty years since my friend showed me where his dad kept a box of magazines full of pictures of naked women, and yet that remains one of the most vivid and formative memories of my childhood. I can remember exactly where we were standing in the garage, where the box was stored, and the rush and sudden warmth I felt as my eyes were opened. It is seared into me like a slaver's brand. I spent years of my life chasing, but never quite capturing, the thrill of that first high. (*High* is the scientifically accurate word for what I felt—scientists have found that porn lights up the same parts of the brain as drugs do.)[11]

I also remember the shame and guilt I felt later. My friend let me take a magazine home, and I wrapped it in plastic and buried it in a box in my backyard. Each time I dug up the box, I vowed it was the last. Those pictures shaped my outlook on sex and warped real relationships in my life and the way I looked at women. To this day, I am sad about each woman whose body I've seen and whom I fantasized about being with, each woman I've glued myself to and taken something from.

BE CAREFUL, LITTLE EYES, WHAT YOU SEE

There is truth to the adage that the eyes are the windows to the soul. What you let in through your eyes will work its way inside. Jesus warned us multiple times in the Gospels that our eyes can cause us to sin (Matthew 5:29; 18:9). He spoke about it with one of the most shocking and disgusting pictures in the whole Bible: it would be better to gouge out your eyes than to see and experience hellfire (Matthew

18:9). John told his readers that three different enemies oppose us: "the lust of the flesh, *the lust of the eyes*, and the pride of life" (1 John 2:16, emphasis added).

Remember Achan, who swiped the booty from Jericho and triggered a curse? Here are his words about what happened: "I saw, I coveted, I took, I hid" (Joshua 7:21, author's paraphrase). That is the path to sin pretty much every time: I saw, I coveted, I took, I hid.

That's what happened when Eve disobeyed God's instructions in the garden of Eden, committing the sin that plunged the world into darkness: "So when the woman saw that the tree was good for food, that it was pleasant to the eyes, and a tree desirable to make one wise, she took of its fruit and ate. She also gave to her husband with her, and he ate" (Genesis 3:6). Soon after they were hiding under fig leaves, suddenly aware of and ashamed by their nakedness. I saw, I coveted, I took, I hid.

And it's what happened when David creeped on and became obsessed with Bathsheba, the wife of one of his soldiers. He covered up his lust with the murder of her husband, but his crime began with a look: "Then it happened one evening that David arose from his bed and walked on the roof of the king's house. And from the roof he saw a woman bathing, and the woman was very beautiful to behold" (2 Samuel 11:2). Seeing Bathsheba was a mistake; the sin started when David didn't stop looking. He hadn't done anything wrong until he began coveting. But when he allowed the juices to start flowing, it became very easy to take what wasn't his and eventually shed blood to hide what he had done. I saw, I coveted, I took, I hid.

That is why Job was so wise to make the following arrangement: "I made a covenant with my eyes not to look lustfully at a young woman" (Job 31:1 NIV). We need to make the same covenant, because even if our doors are locked, Satan will come into our lives through open windows. In fact, the devil tried to do exactly that with Jesus during his forty-day temptation in the wilderness: he showed Jesus "all the kingdoms of the world" and promised them in exchange for Jesus' allegiance (Luke 4:5–7).

The reason David failed where Jesus, the Son of David, did not is what they did after they saw what they saw. Jesus looked to God. He quoted a scripture and looked at the temptation through the lens of faith. Because he saw the invisible, he could do the impossible. David, on the other hand, kept looking and soon wanted to hold what he had beheld. It's like binge-watching a TV show on Netflix: the next episode starts automatically in fifteen seconds if you don't act decisively.

We can cut sin off at the pass if we learn not to look at dangerous things in the first place. Knowing a little biology might help: when we see something provocative, our bodies release dopamine and epinephrine, also known as adrenaline. That's why we experience a rush of good feelings, happiness, and a sense of invincibility. One of the reasons pornography is so addictive is because of this "high" that makes you crave more.

The next time your desire is triggered, the craving increases until you give in to it. Like the dog who drools every time a bell rings, you are rewarding and reinforcing a conditioned response every time you give into temptation.

Your brain is always paying attention. Repeated

exposure to sin is how bad habits snowball out of control. Jesus said as much: "Most assuredly, I say to you, whoever commits sin is a slave of sin" (John 8:34). Doing three thousand layups every day won't make you Michael Jordan if you do them with bad form. Practice doesn't necessarily make perfect, but it always makes permanent.

COOLER HEADS PREVAIL

A cheetah can run only until its brain temperature hits 105 degrees Fahrenheit. At that point its options are simple: sit down and pant until it cools down, or die. The gazelle has a chamber where inhaled breath cools down its blood before it gets to the brain. This allows for greater endurance, because the gazelle's body can

Your brain is always paying attention.

be at 109 degrees but its brain will still be at 105.[12] So a gazelle can keep running after the cheetah is forced to stop. This is how a gazelle can escape a cheetah. In the most literal sense, the cooler head prevails.

Shouldn't that be our strategy? Shouldn't we limit access to the kinds of things that get our blood pumping and make our faces flush? And if we do find ourselves faced with temptation, shouldn't we take immediate, aggressive, and evasive action?

I heard a pastor once say to a group of men, "You have only enough blood in your body to power either your brain or your crotch. So if you are thinking with one, the other is not functioning." That potentially offensive—yet highly profound—statement explains so much stupidity in my life and in the lives of people I have known. Stallions have to be kept far away from mares in heat, because the male horses will impale themselves on fences trying to get to the females. Turned-on humans can be as self-destructive as horses. When we hear of people who have made messes of their lives, marriages, careers, or ministries due to sexual sin, we all wonder, *What were they thinking?*

They weren't. Had they thought about their actions, they would have realized that no matter how good what they were about to do was going to feel, it wasn't worth what they would be giving up. Sin makes you stupid.

I once toured the Apple headquarters in Cupertino, California, and the Facebook headquarters in Menlo Park, California. The man who showed us around Apple was one of the people who invented Siri. He and a Facebook employee attended a church where I had spoken, and they invited us into their respective magical kingdoms. I was Charlie, and I had received not one but two golden tickets!

As a card-carrying Apple fanboy, I was nerding out big-time going into Apple's headquarters. I realize it might be going a bit far, but I almost felt like I needed to take my shoes off because I was standing on holy Cupertino ground. (Can you say iDolatry?) But it was something I saw at the Facebook campus that left the biggest mark on me. The items in their vending machines were not labeled with their cost in dollars, as everything was free. Instead, the labels told their true cost: what it would take to burn off the food (for example: Snickers bar—twenty-five-minute bike ride).

I marveled at the wisdom. The food might be "free," but it still costs you something. Nothing is truly free in this world. Weighing in the true cost of our choices is an incredibly powerful way to combat temptations that seem appealing in the moment. Nothing cools my head down faster than thinking about doing burpees. I don't eat healthy because I like it; I eat healthy because I hate doing cardio.

Remember what I told you in chapter 1: *now* yells louder, but *later* lasts longer. Nothing will cut through an overheating brain faster than a few well-placed questions about whether an hour of sinful pleasure is worth your job or the respect of your children. In business they talk about weighing the opportunity cost of decisions. We would be wise to consider what opportunities our choices will cost us down the road.

> Weighing in the true cost of our choices is an incredibly powerful way to combat temptations that seem appealing in the moment.

WHEN ALL ELSE FAILS, RUN!

Limiting your access to temptation is the most straightforward way to avoid sin. But it is incredibly smart to have a plan in your back pocket in case of emergency. I suggest the following: when all else fails, *run!*

You can memorize Scripture, limit what you watch and read, and generally avoid temptation, but sometimes you'll just get blindsided. There will come a day when you are trying to do the right thing, but all of a sudden, temptation smacks into you.

This happened to Joseph, my boy from the OT. Joseph had a hard life. He was sold into slavery by his older brothers. Every older brother has thought about it, but his went through with it! He ended up in Egypt, where he worked for one of Pharaoh's government officials, Potiphar (Genesis 37:28, 36). No matter what challenges Joseph faced, he sought God and refused to swipe wrong. He could have said, "I'm gonna do what I want and have a good time. God doesn't care about me." But he didn't. He knew that his life didn't have to be going right in order for him to live right.

And then one day Potiphar's wife came to him and said, "Hey, Joseph! I think you're super good-looking. Let's have sex!" And he's like, "Whoa! Whoa! What the heck? No, I'm not going to have sex with you! That would be wrong. Wrong against your husband and wrong in the eyes of God" (Genesis 39:7–9, author's paraphrase). But she wasn't easily discouraged. She propositioned him over and over (v. 10), but Joseph wouldn't have any of it. He went out of his way to avoid her.

So she stalked him. And once he was alone in the house, she made her move. She grabbed him by his jacket and said, "Let's have sex right now! I'm not letting go of you until you take me" (Genesis 39:11–12, author's paraphrase). By the way, this story is especially crazy because Joseph's dad back in Israel thought Joseph was dead. Joseph's brothers said Joseph had been killed by a wild animal, but the truth was, he was actually in Egypt, getting mauled by a cougar. The whole situation is very *Real Housewives of the Ancient World*.

Here's what Joseph didn't do: he didn't say, "You know what? Let's pray about this." Instead, Joseph jumped out of his jacket and ran away. He *ran*. Why? Because he knew if he stayed in that house for one red-hot minute, he might have given in. So he got out of there.

And you must do the same. When you begin to feel tempted to watch what you shouldn't watch, do what you shouldn't do, or go where you shouldn't go, then it's time to go all 2 Timothy 2:22: "Flee also youthful lusts." I love that verse, because the word translated "flee" is the Greek word *pheugo*. P-H-E-U-G-O: when you are in a situation where you are faced with temptation, "Foo," you just got to "go!" There's some gangster in the Greek.

Close the computer, cancel your cable, walk out of the movie (they will probably even refund your ticket price if you ask), delete the contact from your phone, break up with that person, change schools, or quit your job if you have to. Pluck out the eye, cut off the hand. Do something drastic to your sin, or sin will do something drastic to you. I know this all sounds way intense—and maybe it is—but know this: you can't have a healthy soul and mainline toxic substances. "Keep your heart with all diligence, / For out of it spring the issues of life" (Proverbs 4:23). You are what you eat. What you feed on, you'll be full of.

Put down the Red Bull and go to bed. You can thank me in the morning.

CHAPTER 8

Samson's Hair Began to Grow

When I was in high school, a friend broke one of my two front teeth. It was a major fiasco, and as recently as this week, the tooth is a source of pain, inconvenience, embarrassment—and expense.

The fight involved a girl. (Isn't it always about a girl?)

My friend, the girl, and I were standing around in a lobby. My friend made a joking motion as though he was going to fight her, and, in a grand over-the-top display of chivalry, I stepped between them and said, "If you want to get to her, you will have to go through me first."

He accepted the challenge, took a step back, and removed the windbreaker he had thrown over his shoulder. Then he gestured toward me with it as though it was going to be the ceremonial glove slap before a duel. In good fun I offered my cheek, unafraid to fight for the lady's honor. I should have stayed out of it.

As my friend swung the jacket toward me, neither of us considered that the jacket's zipper pull—a metallic Nike logo—was racing at me too. He pulled back before the jacket hit my face, but as he did, the flick of his wrist caused that little zipper pull to jerk like a bullwhip and connect with tooth 8, my right maxillary central incisor.

My tooth shattered.

It took a moment to realize what had happened. Both my friend and the girl stared at me with eyes bulging out of their heads like in a Snapchat filter. My tongue found its way to the tooth, and I assessed the damage. All that remained was a little stump.

My buddy felt terrible. It was just an unfortunate accident, and I forgave him immediately, but the damage was done. If only it were a better story. If only I had been in a skydiving accident or a bar fight or had been attacked by a velociraptor. No, my smile was permanently altered by a zipper pull featuring a logo that was designed for thirty-five dollars.

So began two decades of dental work. First the dentist added a bonding that looked very untoothlike. A year later, the nerve died, and I had to have a root canal. Due to a mix-up in the dental office, the dentist numbed the wrong side of my mouth and began drilling without appropriate anesthetic. My body went rigid, as though I were being electrocuted, and tears streamed down my face. The dentist stopped immediately and realized what had happened. I'll never forget what happened next: with a hand on my shoulder, he said, "Sorry for the fireworks back there, buddy." I wanted to bite his fingers off.

After the root canal, he put on a temporary that looked a lot like a piece of Chiclet gum—it was at least three shades too white. Fortunately, it was on a front tooth that everyone could see all the time. Despite having been through braces, I still had big buckteeth (less-than-kind "friends" in junior high called me RatBoy), so this did not help.

Over the years I have spent thousands of dollars on dental work and have been fitted with different crowns varying in quality. The most recent one was put on this week and is by far the most toothlike in shape, color, and texture. Unlike my last one, which was porcelain-covered metal, this one is solid porcelain; it's thinner, so it sits flush with the rest of my upper teeth. I am very thankful, as the appearance of my smile has always made me self-conscious.

The moral of the story is that you've gotta be careful with your adult teeth, because you get only one set. Treat them kindly, or you'll lose them, and they don't grow back.

Hair works differently. As long as your hair follicles are living, no matter how short you cut your hair, it will keep coming back. No sooner do you shave than that stubborn stubble starts to appear.

ROGAINE FOR YOUR SOUL

Lean in and listen closely: no matter what you have done or how far you have run, you can still experience God's love, power, and plan for you. The life he wants you to live is ever growing and constantly replenishing. It's not one strike and you're out, or three, or seventy times seven. No matter what some grumpy Sunday school teacher with bad breath might have told you, God is not an angry Santa Claus with a lightning bolt, waiting to cut you down to size.

One of my favorite Bible verses is Judges 16:22. Read it very slowly and carefully: "But before long, [Samson's] hair began to grow back" (NLT). This might not seem like much to you, but remember what Samson had done: Samson had drunk out of the devil's Crock-Pot, paying for temporary pleasure with future power. The enemy took Samson's strength and his eyes, and all the man got for it was a few nights with Delilah.

Samson was a judge. Don't think gavel and gown; he was more legionnaire than lawyer. He was supposed to be consecrated (fancy word for dedicated) to God. Samson had to follow some unique rules: he was never supposed to touch anything dead or drink alcohol, and as a symbol of his great strength, his hair was never to be cut. He did some epic things on the battlefield, but he let his appetites drive and ended up crossing every boundary set for him.

Famously, he slept with a woman named Delilah, who was a honey pot used by his enemies to destroy him. He let his guard down and told her his secret—that cutting his hair would make him lose his power—which she told to her bosses. After a quick buzz cut, he was as weak as Superman holding kryptonite.

That's the part of the story that we focus on, but I see the problem beginning much earlier, when he was cruising through a vineyard (Judges 14:5). What was a guy who isn't supposed to drink doing in a vineyard? That's like going to Hooters for the wings. Haven't you ever heard of Chili's? He later saw a beehive in the dead carcass of a lion, and he ate some of the honey. How did he get the honey out? With his hands—but remember, he was never supposed to touch a dead animal. You see, he was playing with fire long before Delilah came around. By the time he had sex with a Philistine and gave away the secret to his strength, he had already desensitized himself with a series of compromises. Most people wreck their lives slowly.

Samson's story should send chills down your spine. It flat-out terrifies me. Seeing someone so gifted, so talented, so strong throw it all away for so little should cause us to wake up and straighten up and take very seriously that one degree off course today could lead us to disaster eventually.

Samson's strength left him when his head was shaved. By the time he realized it was a trap, it was too late. His eyes were poked out. His enemies wrapped him in chains and put him in a mill, where he was made to grind grain. Occasionally they brought him out to laugh at him.

This is all very sad, but there is redemption in it. In those dark days, he came to his senses, and his heart turned to God in prayer. As he did, a little stubble appeared on his scalp. Not much, just some five o'clock shadow on top of his head. Little by little it grew, and as it did, so did he.

I'm not saying everything was as it used to be—he never got his sight back—but as his hair got longer, he became stronger, and with that newfound power came a resolve. His desire was for the enemy to pay for what was taken away. God used Samson more powerfully in his weakness than he had in the rest of Samson's life. The last words out of Samson's mouth were "for my two eyes" (Judges 16:28).

Maybe you, like Samson, feel hopeless. Maybe you lost everyone's trust because of a drug addiction that spiraled out of control. Maybe you showed up for work drunk and it cost you your job. Did you cheat on your spouse and contract a sexually transmitted disease? Did you get kicked out of school after your parents sacrificed to fund your tuition? Are you so low that suicide seems like the best way out?

It's not too late. Your hair can grow again. I've read the Bible from front to back, and while there is a lot I don't understand, this I know: it all works out in the end. That means if it hasn't worked out yet—it isn't the end! As long as your heart is beating in your chest, there remains hope of a better tomorrow. I believe Jesus can restore to you days that sin has eaten.

> As long as your heart is beating in your chest, there remains hope of a better tomorrow.

There can be reconciliation where there was only animosity. There can be trust where there was only suspicion. I have seen marriages that were seemingly over—and then, all of a sudden, they weren't. Never forget we serve a God whose Son was dead—until he wasn't. God can make a way where there is no way. I'm not saying it will be instant, clean, or easy; but if you give God the space to be God, he will bring new stubble from the rubble. He will help you slowly but surely build bridges of trust where there are severed relationships. The name of Jesus is greater than heroin, divorce, debt, addiction, incarceration, prostitution, or bankruptcy. It matters not how deep of a pit you have fallen into or how long you have been there—only whether you are willing to be made well.

Jesus can heal, and maybe he will. He could say the word, and the charges against you could be dropped, the disease could leave your body, or your children could want to be in your life. If God had wanted to, he could have regenerated Samson's eyes. What's so powerful about Samson's story is that his eyes never grew back, but his hair *did*. Even if God doesn't heal or deliver the same way you ask and if some consequences linger, he can work in the midst of the dysfunction to bring about good things. If that is the case—the divorce goes through or the judge throws the book at you—your desire should be like Samson's: to make the devil pay for what he has taken away. How? Whenever you are at your darkest, shine your brightest.

I'M DOING IT RIGHT NOW

I learned the hard way how difficult it is to overcome exposure to pornography. In the technical sense, my wife, Jennie, was the first person I had sex with, but in every other sense, she was not. I wish I hadn't played so fast and loose with my heart and the hearts of those with whom I was intimate.

I can't unsee or undo what I saw or did, but I can share my experience with the generation after me. Because I swiped wrong, I wrote this book to tell you that even though we live in a left/right world, you should look up and swipe right. I find power in sharing my story and my message. If even one person hears my voice and lets my hindsight become his or her foresight, it is worth it. Like Samson, I am making the enemy pay for my two eyes—and so can you.

Maybe this means that one day you will mentor young people who struggle with addiction. Or perhaps you will get involved in a program that provides friendship and love to at-risk children, because those are something you never had. What if the hard things you went through weren't for naught, because someone would hear your stories and be spared heartache? Will you offer debt counseling for families who don't know how to budget or tithe? That future might seem a long way away right now, as you struggle to breathe under a mountain of debt that could cave at any moment. But God has a funny way of using what's monstrously difficult in our lives to be monumentally helpful to other people.

There is a couple in my church who springs to action when they learn of a marriage on the rocks, especially if there has been infidelity. Like an intensive care unit, they do everything they can to nurse the relationship back to health. We have seen God use their ministry in mighty ways.

But years ago, it seemed their own marriage was not going to make it. I remember the tears, the anger, and the sadness they were experiencing when God put it on my heart to tell them that, as impossible as it seemed, they were going to make it. Furthermore, I added, I believed a day would come when we would send couples to them to be ministered to in the very area that seemed to be killing them. Their eyes betrayed their incredulousness and doubt, but here we stand today—they are mighty and strong, and they've made the devil pay for their two eyes.

Proverbs 24:16 says that even if a man falls seven times, he can get back up. In the Bible, the number seven stands for completeness.[1] The verse isn't saying that after the eighth fall, it's over; it's saying that no matter how devastated your life seems, you can still get back up.

Get back up.

Get back up.

Rocky Balboa said, "It ain't about how hard you hit. It's about how hard you can get hit and keep moving forward."[2] The end can be better than the beginning. Samson killed more Philistines as a blind man with a buzz cut than he ever did in the glory days of his youth. He had something at the end he never had at the beginning—humility.

I'M NOT WORTHY TO BE CALLED YOUR CHILD

As you get back up, you'll discover a massive barrier: shame. You will feel unworthy—and you are.

Get over it! Grace isn't merited. You don't honor the Father by groveling or by hanging your head and slumping your shoulders like Eeyore feeling sorry for himself. The Lord doesn't get any pleasure out of your paying penance for things Jesus has already paid for. God, like the father of the prodigal son, wants to give you a signet ring and kill the fatted calf, even though you have rebelled. Your unwillingness—out of principle or guilt—to let him bless you doesn't make him happy. Wear the robe, and dance to the music; he loves you, so let him put a ring on your finger.

One of the most encouraging verses you'll ever read is Jeremiah 29:11. It's one of the first verses I remember reading. Odds are good you have read it while relieving yourself, as it is a verse that, oh, about 73 percent of Christian homes and churches have hanging on a plaque in the bathroom: "For I know the thoughts that I think toward you, says the LORD, thoughts of peace and not of evil, to give you a future and a hope."

You might be familiar with this uplifting verse, but I would say that most of us are not getting out of it all the encouragement it offers. It is one of those passages that has been hijacked from its context and isolated as a gem with no thought as to the surrounding verses that explain what Jeremiah was actually responding to.

Let me paint the backstory for you.

Jeremiah ministered before and during the Babylonian captivity (Jeremiah 1:1–3), when the Israelites near Jerusalem lost their lands to Nebuchadnezzar (as their fellow tribes in Samaria had over a century earlier to Assyria). The politically powerful people from Judah and Benjamin were exiled to Babylonia. The captivity happened for one reason. God's number one rule is "You shall have no other gods before Me" (Exodus 20:3), and the remaining free Israelites had begun to worship the gods and adopt the traditions of their pagan neighbors.

God gave the Israelites a lot of mercy. Prophet after prophet had warned them over and over again to return to right worship, but they didn't listen. God won't make us obey; we have free will. God doesn't treat you like a robot or a doll with a string that he pulls to make you love him.

At the point when Jeremiah wrote, they were waking up in Babylon, hungover and coming to terms with what they had done. They had made their beds, and now they had to sleep in them. I imagine they felt regret, shame, hopelessness, and despair.

In that moment God inspired Jeremiah to deliver an important message:

> For thus says the LORD: After seventy years are completed at Babylon, I will visit you and perform My good word toward you, and cause you to return to this place. For I know the thoughts that I think toward you, says the LORD, thoughts of peace and not of evil, to give you a future and a hope. Then you will call upon Me and go and pray to Me, and I will listen to you. And you will seek Me and find Me, when you search for Me with all your heart. (Jeremiah 29:10–13)

Have you ever made a mistake and then felt instant regret and remorse? In this new digital world, it's easier than ever to put your foot in your mouth publicly. We can now wreck our lives in 140 characters or less.

The *New York Times* describes how one woman "blew up" her life in "one stupid tweet."[3] Before boarding an international flight, Justine Sacco posted to her Twitter feed something racially insensitive and politically incorrect that she thought would be funny to her friends. She never thought anyone else would see it, because she had only 170 followers. By the time her flight landed, her name was the number one worldwide trending topic. She had received death threats and was being publicly shamed all over the globe. She soon lost her job. Someone even waited at the airport and photographed her arrival to try to catch her reaction when she took her phone out of airplane mode.

Sacco said, "I cried out my body weight in the first 24 hours. . . . It was incredibly traumatic. You don't sleep. You wake up in the middle of the night forgetting where you are."[4]

USA Today ran a story about a man who uploaded a video to YouTube in which he is inexplicably ranting to a woman working a Chick-fil-A drive-through. When the video went viral, the Internet turned on him. By the time he got back to work at a pharmaceutical company he had been fired, losing his two-hundred-thousand-dollar salary and a million dollars in stock options. He is now living on food stamps, unable to find employment, because whenever potential employers Google him, they see the video.[5]

We've all done things that have made us wish we could hit Command-Z and make the whole mess disappear. So we have a taste of how the Israelites felt as they were coming to their senses in captivity. Imagine their remorse as the consequences of their disobedience set in. They had come full circle. Remember that God had gone to tremendous lengths to deliver them from slavery in Egypt and bring them to the promised land: he sent the ten plagues, he parted the Red Sea, he provided manna to eat, he made the sun stand still.

The Israelites had *one job*, but they had systematically dismantled

> We've all done things that have made us wish we could hit Command-Z and make the whole mess disappear.

the force field that kept them safe. God had promised no one would be able to oppose them if they kept their hearts toward him but that they would lose power without his strong hand (Joshua 23). By ignoring God's repeated warnings, they lowered the shield they had in God and were vulnerable as the Babylonians laid siege. Like Samson after his haircut, the Israelites found out how weak they were when God took their strength away. Once again they found themselves in a foreign land, slaves to another cruel king—with no one to blame but themselves. They had sabotaged themselves and were rightly down in the dumps about it.

I imagine they felt even worse when Jeremiah's message arrived. They were probably expecting a big, fat "I told you so"—the literary equivalent of a dog getting its nose rubbed in the carpet. How shocking instead to find that the message contained an invitation to the life they were born to live. Essentially it said, "God's got big plans for you. There is a calling on your life. It's not too late. You're not too far gone."

It wasn't shame but hope that marked the tone of this message. That's how our God rolls: "Through the LORD's mercies we are not consumed, / Because His compassions fail not. / They are new every morning; / Great is Your faithfulness" (Lamentations 3:22–23). No matter what you have done, where you have been, what mistakes you've made or what they've cost you—

whether a marriage has ended,

your company has gone under,

your grown children won't talk to you,

your sexual decisions have left you numb inside,

or you are addicted to a substance that consumes you—

God has plans for you!

That's the message of the Bible. And if Scripture teaches us anything, it's that in God's hands dead things can come back to life. There's always hope for a new beginning. The word *hopeless* isn't in God's vocabulary.

You might feel as if you are in a valley of dry bones. (If you're familiar with the Bible, think Ezekiel 37; if you are more familiar with *The Lion King*, think of the elephant graveyard.) All around you is tragedy you weren't prepared for, conflict you didn't ask for, bills you can't pay for, and trials you didn't plan for.

In Jesus' name, those dry bones can live. God can breathe on dust to create a man, and the Spirit that raised Christ from the dead can reanimate the pieces of your broken dreams. Don't give up, no matter how bad things seem! Remember this: "The Spirit of God, who raised Jesus from the dead, lives in you. And just as God raised Christ Jesus from the dead, he will give life to your mortal bodies by this same Spirit living within you" (Romans 8:11 NLT).

Easter was never meant to be a once-a-year holiday but rather an everyday reality. You can open up a can (or a six-pack) of Easter any time you want. The more desperate your case, the more space there is for God's grace! He wants you to know better days are on their way.

As Jeremiah put it, God wants to give you a *future* and a *hope*. Translation: He wants to move you forward to a better tomorrow. That's the definition of hope: confident expectation that something good will happen. With God you are never stuck where you are. Proverbs 4:18 says, "The path of the just is like the shining sun, / That shines ever brighter unto the perfect day."

God told the Israelites they would be brought back from Babylonia to Jerusalem. Returning to the promised land would be the equivalent of Samson's hair growing back. The word *Jerusalem* means "city of peace": *jeru* (city) + *salem* (peace). The Hebrew idea of peace wasn't just the absence of war. *Shalom* is total wholeness, inside and outside— complete blessing. God was saying, "You're going to live in the city of peace once more!"

We live in a day when people are desperate for hope. Many have had things taken from them, and hope leaves them too. Remember how one out of five women are sexually assaulted while in college? Research shows that more than 65 percent of victims never report the offense to police,[6] because outing yourself as a rape victim can be social suicide. Those whom I have talked with feel as though they've been kidnapped and will never get back to the city of peace.

Maybe you can relate. Perhaps right now it doesn't seem possible to ever stop hurting, to lose weight, or to get out of debt.

We brand ourselves and give ourselves permanent labels: *I'm a divorcée, I'm an orphan, I declared bankruptcy, I am a felon*—or even something as simple as *I'm not a morning person*—as though that is what we will always be. But the power of the cross is that your identity doesn't come from your activity or your life's brutality, but from the perfect love of Jesus. You are not defined by your failures or pain, but by his forgiveness.

BEAUTIFY YOUR BABYLON

The power of the cross is that your identity doesn't come from your activity or your life's brutality, but from the perfect love of Jesus.

If you are in Christ, you are a new creation; old things have passed away (2 Corinthians 5:17, author's paraphrase). Your life has that new-car smell! You are chosen, you are loved, you are called, and you are equipped. You are God's masterpiece.

I dare you to believe you won't always hurt as you do right now. There will come a day when you'll no longer feel like an empty shell of a person. Channel that Biggie Smalls vibe—"You're going, going back, back to Salem, Salem!"

And in the meantime? He wants you to flourish right where you are. Restoration takes time. All that the Israelites forfeited would be redeemed, but it wouldn't happen immediately. Read carefully what God said: "After *seventy years* are completed at Babylon, I will . . . perform My good word toward you, and cause you to return to this place" (Jeremiah 29:10, emphasis added).

This hope delayed speaks to the reality of consequences that remain. Forgiveness is comprehensive, but it isn't a get-out-of-jail-free card. Legal problems, pregnancy, loss of trust, videos preserved online for eternity—these can be the new normal that can't be ignored. This sounds discouraging, but it should encourage you—God's not committed to you for a weekend but for a lifetime. You are going to have to go through it, but you won't be alone. Even if it takes seventy years to get back to Jerusalem, he'll be with you every day you spend in Babylon.

What are you supposed to do until then? Flourish right where you are. Earlier in Jeremiah 29, God gave the Israelites marching orders for their seventy-year stint in Babylon. It's helpful to every one of us who can't get the toothpaste of our mistakes back in the tube: "Build houses and dwell in them; plant gardens and eat their fruit. . . . And seek the peace of the city where I have caused you to be carried away captive, and pray to the LORD for it; for in its peace you will have peace" (vv. 5, 7).

I love this! God is saying that if you can't live in the city of peace, bring peace to the city you live in. Don't endure it—enjoy it! Plant a garden. Eat some fruit. Build a house. Make the home you live in better. Give comfort to other people. Beautify your Babylon! Some roses over here would be nice. Landscaping that walkway could be cool.

I know this advice is super difficult to follow. But what if you focus on your walk with God and build up your heart? What if you plant some righteous seeds? How about getting a gym membership and listening to podcasts that build your soul while you work on your body? Maybe you should go to a retirement home and hang out with people who have no one to play cards with. Bloom where you are planted.

Don't just mourn for what you have lost; change what you can. God wants you to flourish right where you are! He's so good he'll bless you in places you never should have gone. Samson was used by God to defeat Israel's enemies while he was in prison. He could have sulked and died a victim, but he made it his goal to do what he could where he was for God's cause.

You can't live the life you gave up, so live the life you have.

And whatever you do, *don't give up*! Seeds take time to grow.

When we ripped out a dead tree in our front yard, a bare spot appeared in our lawn. After a quick trip to Lowe's, we came home with a bag labeled "Bare Spot Repair." Being a brilliant delegator, I decided this would be the perfect project for my kids. Alivia dutifully read the instructions and involved her sisters in putting down the new soil, scattering the seeds, and watering them. After about twenty minutes, the girls came inside and announced the job was done. I went outside with Alivia and Clover to inspect the work, but my middle child, Daisy, lagged behind in the house. As I praised my daughters, Daisy came running out toward us, singing the question, *"Did it grow? Did it grow? Did it grow?"* When she got to us, she saw there was no new grass shooting out of the ground, and her face fell. Disappointment stretched from ear to ear as she walked away.

I couldn't help but laugh at her logic and see myself in her impatience. She had planted and watered seeds and assumed there would be immediate change. If only real life worked as it did in "Jack and the Beanstalk." We give twenty years to the devil and two weeks to God, and then expect everything to change overnight. God doesn't offer Amazon Prime, and there isn't a drone that can drop-ship sanctification. You've just got to do the hard yards of walking with Jesus. We are so used to Starbucks Via and microwavable Hot Pockets that we think there should be a spiritual shortcut. But growing fruit takes time and flourishing takes work. In its time God will do it swiftly (Isaiah 60:22).

If you think it's taking forever, don't get impatient, get praying. To a seed, being planted feels a lot like being buried; but if you wait and water and wait some more, what went down will come up. In the meantime roll with it like the Penguins of Madagascar: "Smile and wave, boys. Smile and wave."

CHAPTER 9

Vice President Biden in My Bed

My graduation from high school was a lie. I wore a cap and gown, and my family all came to watch, take pictures, and cheer when my name was called. I walked the stage, moved my tassel, and threw my hat with all my classmates; but it was all as genuine as a Louis Vuitton purse bought on Canal Street.

The situation was a matter of economics. To be technical, the problem was laziness, but it finally caught up with me my senior year in economics class. Throughout high school, I was never one to hit the books at home. As long as I had a study hall (why burden myself with a cumbersome elective course such as trigonometry?) I could get most of my work done during the school day. Even though I never studied, I found I could skate through tests with passing grades. Public speaking came especially easy to me from a young age. Reading and creative arts were enjoyable, and I had no problem knocking out book reports or writing papers. Math not so much.

Senioritis bit me hard in twelfth grade, and I found myself doing even less of the bare minimum. I realized that there was very little that could change the solid but rather unimpressive streak of Bs and Cs I had racked up over four years of not applying myself. Looking back, I think of certain teachers who tried to inspire me to apply myself, telling me about my potential and how I could be on the honor roll or make straight As if I would just try. But I refused. If you had asked me, I would have tried to play off a clever quote from the movie *Fight Club*: "I am Levi's complete lack of surprise."[1] Or said something about busywork being meaningless, or bemoaned the fact that chances were none of it would ever be useful in real life and that I am more than the khaki pants the school made me wear.

Yeah, I was that guy. I was also wrong.

One of the first things I did after signing a book deal with my publisher was to go straight to Google and type, "What is a semicolon?" I figured as long as I was going to be an author of a book, I might as well find out. Other things I never mastered in all my years of formal education include how to write the entire cursive alphabet (my Qs, Zs, and Xs are Billy Madison–style), how to multiply fractions, and what to do when using an apostrophe on a word that ends with an *s*. The horror.

I genuinely liked my senior-year economics teacher. Her name was Mrs. Bellomy, and she was a no-nonsense lady with a sense of humor who would tell us exactly how it was in a way that I respected. She was originally from Seattle, and I remember her telling us stories about when Mount Saint Helens blew and how much she couldn't stand living in a city without a Nordstrom. Sadly, I can't tell you too much about our nation's economy, but volcanos and shopping I remember. She made a genuine impression on me, and I appreciated her more than I probably let on.

One day she pulled me aside after class to warn me that, because of some incomplete assignments, I was running the risk of failing the class. This had never happened to me before, but I assured her I would be able to raise my grade in time.

At the time I had a part-time job busing tables from dinner to closing, and I was dating a college student. None of this did anything to keep me focused on my studies. *Scholastically checked out* is how I would describe my frame of mind.

Everything came to a head when Mrs. Bellomy made good on her threats and failed me when I missed one more piece of "busywork." Things got real when I was called into the office for a meeting and informed that I would not be able to graduate high school without the credit.

I am Levi's cold sweat.

I begged, I pleaded, I shed tears. In the end, we reached a very gracious compromise. I would be allowed to walk with my graduating class, and I would be handed a diploma case like all the other students, only there would be no diploma in it. I could retake economics via distance learning over the summer, and if I completed it in time, I'd get my diploma in the mail. This, my friend, is called mercy.

I will never forget how I felt that day when I walked across that stage, shook my principal's hand, and looked him in the eye as he gave me an expression that communicated volumes. None of my friends, nor those in the audience, had a clue what was really going on. My parents did, and though they never said as much, I'm sure they were disappointed. Proverbs 10:1 says, "A wise son makes a glad father, / but a foolish son is the grief of his mother." They had echoed what teachers had been saying at parent-teacher conferences and writing on report cards my whole life: I had so much untapped potential, and if I would only apply myself, I could do something great with my life. To their credit, both my parents always encouraged me to find my passion and pursue it, whether or not that included college.

I didn't need anyone to shame me to feel bad. I knew the truth, and I didn't like how it felt. The emptiness of the ceremony was matched by a hollowness I felt at the meaninglessness of a job not well done. *Way to go!* I thought. *You phoned in high school and got away with it, but the joke's on you, because you didn't get out of it anything close to what you could have.*

The experience profoundly impacted me, and from then on I committed to apply myself. Excellence has become a cultivated passion that I now find great fulfillment in. The bare minimum is no longer my go-to, and I have learned to enjoy going above and beyond no matter what I am working on. I'm trying to impart this virtue to my children as well. One of the "core values" of our family is that whatever we do, we do with all our hearts. Even if a task seems insignificant, or if we think we'll never need to do it later in life, if what we're doing is to the glory of God, it's worth being done right.

LOOKS CAN BE DECEIVING

I should tell you, dear reader, that I have never shared this part of my story publicly before. The first rule of not graduating high school is: You don't talk about not graduating high school. In case you're wondering why I'm divulging it fifteen years after the fact (especially because this book is supposed to be about relationships), my thinking is twofold: First, it's cheaper than therapy, and it felt good to get it off of my chest. Second, I want you to keep that image of my empty diploma case in your mind, because looks can be deceiving. Everyone crowded into the chairs at my high school graduation saw what they wanted to see. But just because I was wearing a cap and gown and holding a diploma case didn't mean I was actually graduating.

Bringing this idea back around to relationships—I can't stress this next sentence strongly enough: *It's easier than you think to marry a stranger.*

There once was a man who woke up the morning after his wedding to quite a surprise: the woman next to him was not his wife but his wife's sister. The man was Jacob—the same Jacob from chapter 1, who made the stew and stole his brother's birthright. Let's backtrack and pick up the story where we left off earlier.

Esau was furious. Not only had Jacob swindled him out of the birthright, but he had also tricked their father into giving him the ceremonial blessing that should have gone to Esau. Esau had had enough. He was prepared to kill his younger brother, and he probably thought he could get the birthright and the blessing back once Jacob was dead.

Their mom learned of Esau's plans and knew she had to act fast. She asked her husband, Isaac, for permission to send Jacob away to find a wife, even though they both knew it wasn't necessary: God had orchestrated Rebekah and Isaac's coming together without either of them going out on the hunt, and he would have been faithful to do the same for Jacob.

Nonetheless, off Jacob went to play the field and hopefully not get murdered in the process. He set off into the wilderness. It was quickly apparent that he was not suited for life in the wild when he set up camp and used a rock as a pillow (Genesis 28:11). I'm certainly no Bear Grylls, but even I know that this was not a solid plan.

The beautiful thing is that God met Jacob where he was. Jacob had a dream that he didn't fully understand in the moment, but it began to change him so he no longer felt the need to scheme and cheat to get ahead, instead trusting in God to lead and guide him.

Eventually he arrived at a place called Padan Aram and met a relative named Laban. What comes next is so shocking and unbelievable I want to let you read it exactly as the Bible described it: "Now Laban had two daughters; the name of the older was Leah, and the name of the younger was Rachel. Leah had weak eyes, but Rachel had a lovely figure and was beautiful" (Genesis 29:16–17 NIV).

I will interrupt here to let you know that "weak eyes" is not a compliment. To introduce someone as having weak eyes and then quickly change subjects to talk about her beautiful sister? Ouch. For her sake it's a good thing the book of Genesis wasn't written while Leah was alive.

Interestingly I wrote this chapter in an upscale, super hip coffee shop in the design district of Dallas. That night I was speaking at an event at AT&T Stadium, where the Cowboys play, but I stole a couple of hours to continue work on this book, which I had told my publisher would be done by then (insert grimacing clenched teeth emoji). This swanky boutique establishment brews single-origin pour-over coffees by the cup, describing the options with phrases like "it has a chocolaty mouth feel" or "a pomegranate finish." Once the sun sets, they sell wine with the same verbiage. It's full of trendy people and smells like money. There was a film crew shooting on the corner, and as I was ordering I saw a man sipping a latte while the director instructed him to keep drinking and ignore the camera.

I took a seat outside on the patio to write. At one point the cameraman came outside and scanned the crowded tables. Twice he looked straight at me, but then he moved on and approached other people to ask permission to film them while they ate or drank. After filming several others, he looked once more at me and obviously determined me to be weak on the eyes before going back inside. Apparently I was not ready for my close up . . . or maybe it was my sweatpants. (Don't judge me. You don't know what I've been through.)

The moment Jacob saw Rachel he fell for her:

Jacob was in love with Rachel and said [to Laban], "I'll work for you seven years in return for your younger daughter Rachel."

Laban said, "It's better that I give her to you than to some other man. Stay here with me." So Jacob served seven years to get Rachel, but they seemed like only a few days to him because of his love for her. (vv. 18–20 NIV)

This is one of the most romantic passages in the Bible. Doesn't your heart just melt to think of Jacob skipping through seven years of hard labor as though they were just days? Time flew for him because he was so excited to be with her.

Just to be clear, I found the exact opposite to be true when I met Jennie halfway through her commitment to the Lord not to date anyone for a year. I had made no such oath. I was single and ready to mingle. She caught my eye and made it clear she was interested in only friendship until the year was over. The following six months were absolute torture for me, as I was smitten with a capital S. I'm talking head-over-heels lovesick for her. I listened to a lot of Dashboard Confessional and made angsty entries in my journal. Looking back on that time, though, I am so very thankful for it. It gave us no choice but to build the foundation of friendship that our marriage is based on, without the distraction of something physical that could become a cheap substitute for actual interaction. I highly recommend it.

Once you are married, even if you have a banging sex life and make love for an hour every single day of the week (that exhausts me just to type it!), there will still be twenty-three hours of the day when you are not having sex. The problem I see with so many people's approach to dating is that they seem to prepare for only what will amount to a very small percentage of the time spent married. The benefit of having a good friendship in the early stages without any accompanying physical affection is that it will give you something to do the other twenty-three hours of the day. Sex is like the cherry on top of a sundae. Don't get me wrong—sex is a lot of fun, but no one builds a sundae on top of a cherry. You want a solid foundation of ice cream under that maraschino.

Back to Jacob and Rachel:

> Then Jacob said to Laban, "Give me my wife. My time is
> completed, and I want to make love to her." (v. 21 NIV)

Well, that's pretty blunt, Jacob. Tell us what's *really*
on your mind there, buddy. Just when we were oohing and
ahhing at the-years-seemed-like-days stuff, we see what
you're actually thinking about. Now that Rachel was about
to be Jacob's, all his Hallmark-inspired lines wore off, and
he basically turned into Tarzan, grunting "Me Jacob, you
Rachel."

> So Laban brought together all the people of the place and
> gave a feast. (v. 22 NIV)

We don't know a lot about the wedding. The text doesn't
indicate whether or not Laban booked a DJ or had a fancy
cake. We do, however, know that there was an open bar and
that the beer flowed like wine. I realize all that the text says
is that there was "a feast"—there's no explicit mention of
liquor—but please notice the next verse:

> But when evening came, he took his daughter Leah
> and brought her to Jacob, and Jacob made love to her.
> (v. 23 NIV)

How drunk do you have to be not to notice that the
woman you are making love to is not the one you just married? Brutal.

And Laban gave his servant Zilpah to his daughter as her attendant.

When morning came, there was Leah! So Jacob said to Laban, "What is this you have done to me? I served you for Rachel, didn't I? Why have you deceived me?" (vv. 24–25 NIV)

Interestingly, Jacob's name is synonymous with cheating. You might say that the Trickster has been tricked. The heel-catcher's heel has been caught. The contents of Jacob's gory box, long suppressed and forgotten about, have come back to haunt him. "What a man sows, the same shall he reap" (Galatians 6:7, author's paraphrase).

Even though cultures have changed, and thousands of years have passed, and things are done very differently than in Jacob's day, the exact same thing could happen to you. You could think you're marrying Rachel, but wake up one day and realize you are hitched to Leah.

And not because your shady father-in-law played a trick on you. You could end up living with a stranger, even though you are with the same physical person you married. As time passes, and the fog of deception lifts, you might discover that what was on the package wasn't the same as what was hiding deep down on the inside.

CURB YOUR APPEAL

Lest you come to your senses long after the vows have been said: being married to the wrong person is *much* worse than not being married. To avoid this heartbreakingly common outcome, you've got to start seeing people the way God sees them. To borrow language from my first book, it's essential that you date through the eyes of a lion, not looking at people superficially. Why? Because the most important parts of a person don't show up in a selfie.

Samuel learned this lesson the hard way. God gave him the assignment of finding the next king of Israel after Saul was rejected. Saul was handsome and tall but that's about all. There are a lot of superficially attractive people just like him out there: bulging biceps, big breasts, banging bank accounts, but nothing where it counts. It's easy to hide an ugly heart behind a beautiful face. Saul didn't obey the voice of God, and at the end of the day, nothing is more important than that. God honors those who honor him.

For this job of being a one-man monarch selection committee, God sent Samuel to Bethlehem, to the house of Jesse. All of Jesse's sons were trotted out before this last judge of Israel. As soon as he saw the oldest one, Samuel clicked "Buy it now!" in his mind. He was sold. Jesse's oldest boy was strong and impressive, just as Saul had been. God whispered to Samuel's heart, "Do not look at his appearance or at his physical stature, because I have refused him. For the LORD does not see as a man sees; for man looks at the outward appearance, but the LORD looks at the heart" (1 Samuel 16:7). God sees what can't be seen with the naked eye.

The one son who really *was* king material hadn't even been invited to the party. He was out in the backyard tending sheep. He didn't look like much, but God saw what Jesse and Samuel couldn't. Your heavenly father is comfortable with fixer-uppers. He has never been tricked by curb appeal and bought a lousy foundation. He sees the potential in a rehab property, so long as it's got good bones. What God saw in David that lit him up wasn't height but heart. Saul had been strong, but he was as stubborn as the missing donkeys he had been looking for the day he was anointed king. David was weak and unimpressive, like the sheep he took care of, but that would give him humility and the mind of a shepherd.

That story allows me to write this: maybe the person you're actually meant to marry isn't even someone you're considering because you put together a wish list of qualities you're looking for in a spouse that doesn't include the parts of that person that are actually the most significant. If you hear that and think, *But Levi, you don't understand—the person I want is so hot!*—well, so is hell. Every one of us will get ugly on the outside as we get old and slowly decompose, but if you marry someone who is beautiful within, that beauty remains. Compassion, kindness, generosity— like fine wine, these characteristics get better with time.

SLOW IS SMOOTH, SMOOTH IS FAST

The easiest way to marry the wrong person is to rush. Dating is all about putting your best foot forward. No one's going to walk into the first date and tell you, "I snore and I lie and I'm pretty lazy." I heard the prolific relationship guru Tommy Nelson put it this way: "Dating is marketing;

courtship is 'the close.'"[2] The faster the rush to the altar, the less likely the truth will come out. It's going to take time for someone's real story to emerge. It's exhausting to suck yourself in and wear Spanx—physically and emotionally. If you let your relationship breathe, you're going to see your partner angry. Does Mr. Right turn into Mr. Hulk when he doesn't get his way? Does she handle stress by spending money? Is he good with kids?

If you rush into marriage, you're giving yourself no opportunity to catch your partner in moments that are going to expose his or her true colors. It takes time to see if she is a Leah pretending to be Rachel or not.

Why is it so tempting to rush things forward? Because infatuation is easily mistaken for love. When you are infatuated with someone, you lose your mind. It's like that scene in *Bambi* when everyone gets twitterpated. You get love drunk, and the effect is so powerful that it's spellbinding. The sound of music is in the air, and you just want to run through a field toward each other in slow motion.

You don't want any of your friends around anymore. You don't want to go to work. You feel like saying, "We don't need money, baby. We have love. We will just hold each other."

It sounds really romantic, and it's easy to get caught up in it all. People who are otherwise rational act like fools when they're in love. Rushing to Vegas or the courthouse—or at the very least moving in together—seems like the right thing to do.

These feelings are good things. They're just not *enough* to build a life on. You need to let enough life pass for some of the infatuation to cycle through a little bit. No one can sustain that high forever; it would kill you. Instead, date each other long enough for the fireworks and chemistry to either dissipate or mature. To do that, you have to come to a place where you realize the person you're dating isn't perfect. Then you can either move on or choose to commit to loving who that person really is, not just who you see him or her to be through the steam coming off of the newness of the relationship.

A lot of people who realize they married Leah just didn't see it because they had their oogly-goggles on. If you make the mistake of taking your relationship to a physical level where you are bumping and grinding and making out all crazy, you perpetuate the infatuation. You have tampered with your objectivity. In a dating relationship, where sex begins, sound judgment ends.

Sex is not only a gift that binds two people together; it is also meant to blind you to your partner's faults. Sex releases happy hormones; your eyes dim a little bit in the haze of intimacy and pleasure. While it's certainly not enough by itself to keep a marriage together, when there is solid friendship at the core, sex serves as the icing on the cake. This physical expression of love makes life beautiful, especially after resolving conflict. (And yes, makeup sex is real and amazing!) When you experience sex prematurely, those same happy hormones can backfire by blinding you to your partner's lack of character or manipulative ways. Low lighting is fine during a dinner party, but it's not ideal when you are doing due diligence before the close.

MEASURE TWICE, CUT ONCE

In the infatuation phase, you can't trust your feelings and you shouldn't rely on the substitute of physical intimacy. So what *do* you do? You need to ask these kinds of questions:

What do the trusted, godly people in my life think of the relationship? I'm not talking about your cousin who has been married three times or the girlfriend who sleeps with everything that moves. I'm talking about your pastor, your small group leader, or your parents, if they're believers. What do they think of the relationship?

You might object, "But they're all wrong. Everyone's against us. It's a conspiracy!" Let me be straight with you: You're not star-crossed lovers. If the people who love you are all saying the same thing, there's a reason. Comments such as, "I don't like the effect he's having on you," or, "She seems to be pulling you away from Christ," act as blinking red lights on the dashboard.

Here's another question: Where and when did you meet, and what do you truly have in common with each other? What's this relationship being built on?

What bait did you attract your partner with? Whatever that bait is, you know your partner has an appetite for it. If you say, "I don't like the people I meet. They're only interested in one thing," then maybe fish in a different pond and use a different bait. If you don't like what you're attracting, do something to attract someone else. The club is a great place to meet someone to hook up with. I think God's house is a great place to meet a man or woman of God to do life with.

Another question to ask is this: Is your relationship before marriage honoring God? Are you taking something from each other that actually belongs to your future husband or wife?

I can hear you now. "Gotcha, Levi! Yes, we're sleeping together; yes, we're living together. But we are going to get married. And once we do, it means what I took was actually already mine. I was just getting it early. Inception!"

To the contrary, you are actually teaching your significant other during your single years whether or not you honor God's standards and boundaries. You are telling the person you love what kind of a husband or a wife you're going to be. If you can't be faithful *before* marriage, why should they think you will be faithful *in* marriage? There will always be forbidden fruit.

Above all else, ask whether your prospective spouse is madly in love with Jesus Christ. Notice you didn't hear me say, "Does your partner claim to be a Christian? Do they go to church with you just so you won't break up?" I'm asking, "Is your partner madly and passionately in love with Jesus Christ as his or her Lord and Savior? Do they want his kingdom to come, his will to be done on earth as it is in heaven?"

If the person you are dating is not in love with Jesus and you are, you need to break up immediately.

I can hear you objecting. "If we break up, they won't get saved. They are so close right now."

To which I say, "You are not the Holy Spirit."

And you're not giving the person you love a good shot of getting saved when you damage your witness by entering into a relationship with someone whose soul is not on fire for Jesus.

The best thing you could do would be to say, "Oh, I'm so sorry. I made a mistake. I want you to give your life to Christ. Right now I'm confusing the issue. I hope you'll still keep coming to church as you said you want to, but your walk needs to be between you and Jesus. You're going to stand before God; I'm going to stand before God. And this is not for us right now."

Then, as time passes—and I mean multiple months or longer—without you as the carrot, if he or she persists in walking with Jesus, you can have a different conversation. If you each surround yourself with godly people, you can re-evaluate the relationship. Maybe God will draw you together as you see that person is genuinely madly in love with Christ. But as long as his or her relationship to God is only a means to an end, it won't be enough to go the distance.

Paul advised, "Do not be unequally yoked together with unbelievers. For what fellowship has righteousness with lawlessness? And what communion has light with darkness?" (2 Corinthians 6:14). You can't possibly be united if you're going toward two different destinations.

How crazy would it be if you were in a car with two GPS units trying to tell you to go to two different places? If Google Maps was trying to get you to Canada while Siri was taking you to Mexico? If you and your partner are headed in two different directions, how do you know which way to turn on Sunday morning: "I want to go to church!" "Let's not." You just got paid; what do you do with the money? "I want to give God my first and my best." "Let's get a boat instead." And how will you raise your children? "I want them to know Jesus." "Let's just raise them to be good people."

Marrying the wrong person isn't even the biggest problem; being the wrong person is. Because when you're not becoming the person God's called you to be, you will attract and desire people who are wrong for you.

> Marrying the wrong person isn't even the biggest problem; being the wrong person is.

So here's a new game plan. Instead of focusing and fixating on finding the right one, channel your energy into being the right one. Pastor Andy Stanley likes to ask, "Are you the person the person you're looking for is looking for?"[3] That godly person you want is looking for the person you are meant to become. As Matthew wrote, "Seek first the kingdom of God and His righteousness, and all these things shall be added to you" (Matthew 6:33).

You can make that decision right now. Say, "I'm going to focus on who I am becoming and the issues in my own heart. I don't want to be a Leah, tricking someone or advertising something that's not actually there. I'm going to seek God and believe he's going to give me more at the end of the day than I could have ever tried to get for myself."

A scene from Genesis 24 was instrumental in Jennie's and my relationship: Jacob's dad, Isaac, was in the fields in the evening. And he lifted his eyes. And there was Rebekah. She lifted her eyes and there was Isaac (vv. 63–64).

Isaac wasn't out there playing the field; he was harvesting the field. I don't know of a better way to meet your wife or husband. Jesus said that the laborers are few but the fields are ripe for harvest (Luke 10:2). Laboring for Jesus should occupy your time in your single years. Give it all you've got! If you simply focus on fulfilling the Great Commission—a mission to go fishin' for souls—I believe that one day you will lift your eyes and see a fellow fisherman or fisherwoman who is as passionate about the field as you are, and it will make sense to fish together. Do what God has called you to do. Run in that lane. Then one day you'll lift up your eyes, and there he or she will be.

That's how it was for Jennie and me. She was serving the Lord; I was serving the Lord. Then one day we decided to serve the Lord together, and that's what we've been doing ever since. We met in the field. We fell in love in the field. We've continued in the field. We are raising our kids in the field. When you delight yourself in the Lord, he gives you the desires of your heart (Psalm 37:4). Don't focus so much on playing the dating game but on reaching the world.

I was reminded of this verse recently when I flew to Los Angeles on a Saturday to preach at a church called Hillsong LA. Jennie wanted to come, but because of a schedule conflict, she wasn't able to fly out until first thing Sunday morning. Her flight landed at LAX just as the first service of the morning was kicking off in downtown LA. Next to my chair was one

> Don't focus on playing the dating game but on reaching the world.

reserved for Jennie, but it wasn't clear whether she would get there before I started preaching. Several songs into the worship set, the band started a song called "Faithfulness." I closed my eyes, raised my hands, and lost myself in the presence of God. The song is about how God is faithful through different seasons, both times of sadness and of joy. All of a sudden my hand grazed someone else's. I opened my eyes, and there was my beautiful wife—eyes closed, hands lifted—singing that song. She hadn't interrupted me or said anything—she just jumped into worship. One moment she wasn't there, and the next thing I knew, she was.

That is a perfect picture of how you want to find your spouse. Find, seek, become. Let God do the adding. He knows the dream of your heart. He put it there. He hasn't destined you for celibacy and given you a dream of a husband or wife just to mess with you. That is not our God. He's a giver of good gifts. Lose yourself in worship, and the next thing you know, there will be a worshipper beside you. You'll never have to take your eyes off of Jesus; you'll be able to worship together.

WHO'S BEEN SLEEPING IN MY BED?

A while back, my family and I stayed at a hotel in Charlotte, North Carolina. While the bellman was bringing our bags to the room, he casually told us that the last guest to stay in this particular room was Vice President Joe Biden. He said it with pride—he had a look in his eye that told me he thought we would be impressed. For some reason, the picture of the vice president's smiling face popped into my head, and it sent a shiver down my spine. (Pause here and Google "Joe Biden smiling" real quick. Yep, that's it. Like the grinning Cheshire Cat.)

I couldn't stop thinking about it. Nothing against him as a person or as an elected official, but I couldn't get him out of my head. I like to pretend that no one else has ever stayed in my hotel rooms before. The less I know, the better. I was doing my best not to touch anything—especially not throw pillows, the comforter, or the shower curtain. I couldn't check out of the room fast enough.

Here's the point: when you get married, ultimately you are sleeping with whomever the person you are marrying has slept with. You are bringing into your bed whomever you have had in your bed as well. The strength of a marriage starts with selection of the right spouse and what baggage you bring into the relationship. Stability, or the lack thereof, is the result of the foundation. We bring all of ourselves and our issues and our pasts into a relationship, so if you live circumspectly, there will be much less to come back and haunt you later. You can cut so many problems off at the pass by living God's way.

Pastor Craig Groeschel remarked, "If you want something different from what everybody else has, then you're going to have to do something different than what everybody else does."[4] What everyone else has is definitely not what I want for my daughters and their children or for you. Over the last forty years, doctors have gone from treating two STDs to more than twenty-five different types.[5] According to the US Centers for Disease and Prevention, one in four teenage girls has an STD.[6] Ten thousand American kids a day get a new STD.[7] It goes without saying, but you won't bring into your marriage bed anything you don't let into your body or your spirit. The monstrosity of sexual intercourse outside marriage is that those who indulge in it are trying to isolate one kind of union (the sexual) from all the other kinds of unions that were intended to go along with it and make up the total union.[8]

Rather than managing future consequences, which is like hacking away at the leaves, you need to aim for the root. Today's decisions are tomorrow's sadness or celebration. Right now you are determining who your spouse wakes up to down the road. Your spouse doesn't have to wake up next to a Leah-in-hiding one day. Keep the veep from your bed. Fight for your spouse even if you have no idea who he or she is. As a Nike ad pointed out, "Yesterday you said tomorrow." Today is the day to put God first. Be who he made you to be. You will attract the right one by protecting the right things. Life attracts life. If you are filling your life with tinder while you're single, it will lead to a forest fire down the road.

CHAPTER 10

Date Your Mate—or the Devil Will Find Someone Who Will

A while back I watched a *60 Minutes* interview with Stephen Spielberg in which he said that he still gets as worried, nervous, and scared about his twenty-seventh movie as he did on his first one. Isn't that amazing? The guy who made *Jaws, E. T.,* and *Indiana Jones* still gets jittery on the job. Speaking of *Jaws*, I found it fascinating when, in the same interview, he said he believes that at least half of the success of *Jaws* should go to the man who wrote the score, a person by the name of John Williams. They have done twenty-five movies together.[1] Spielberg is who we think of when we think of *Jaws*, but would the movie have been so powerful if it hadn't been for that ultra creepy *dun-dun* music that played when Jaws was about to show up? I think not.

Success in marriage, just like in movies, comes from both recognizing and appreciating the contributions of others, especially the stuff that happens behind the scenes. A solid marriage requires never phoning it in or going through the motions, but taking it seriously and applying yourself, heart and soul, day after day and year after year. Spielberg wouldn't be where he is had he coasted.

Marriages often don't burn out; they rust out. It would be great if there were a class you could take or a pill you could swallow or a retreat you could go to that would lead to a healthy, strong relationship, but there isn't. You just have to be willing to keep showing up and giving it your all.

A successful marriage is spelled *W-O-R-K*. If your marriage isn't working, it's probably because you aren't working at it. It's not going to happen by itself. Too often we think passively when we should be thinking actively.

We talk about love as though it were an emotion, when it's really a verb. In Ephesians 5:25, Paul instructed husbands, "Love your wives." People say stuff like "I just fell out of love" or "I just don't love him or her anymore." But when you think of love as a verb, both of those sound ridiculous. What would you say if I told you, "I *just fell out* of my truck?" You'd probably tell me to get back in. What if I said, "I *just don't* pay taxes anymore." You'd look at me as if I were crazy. If you have "fallen out" of love or "just don't" love someone anymore, realize that obedience does not require feelings. Often when we do choose to obey, feelings develop.

Every summer I take my family on a camping trip to Glacier National Park. We pencil it in on our calendar months ahead of time as our annual "Luskos in the wild" expedition. Planning vacations, romantic getaways, and even date nights protects them from being just good intentions that get swallowed up by busyness. You will never *find* time for the most important things in life; you must *make* time.

Marriage must be approached the way you make a fire when camping: what takes only a spark to ignite requires diligent effort to maintain. They don't flourish on their own, and left to themselves, they will dwindle to ash. Fuel must be constantly added in order to achieve a powerful fire. Likewise relationships are not turnkey or maintenance free.

Great marriages require a constant infusion of commitment, tears, and lots and lots of forgiveness. I also happen to agree with Dr. Dre, who once said, "Clear communication. Respect. A lot of laughter. And a lot of orgasms. That's what makes a marriage work."[2] Right on all points!

Having a great marriage is not easy. Very few things in this life that bring true joy are. What success will you find in academics, sports, work, music, science, or literature without paying a price? Easy come, easy go. Great husbands and wives are made, not born.

You will enjoy to the level of your exertion. Marriages are like saving accounts: they have only what you put there through sacrifice over time, but the more you invest and the more patient you are, the more it will pay off.

If you abandon your marriage to start a new relationship, all you are doing is walking across the street to a different bank, opening a new account,

> Marriages are like saving accounts: they have only what you put there through sacrifice over time.

and starting at square one with someone else; your finances stay the same. Compound interest can't ever take hold if you don't leave your investment in one place for an extended time.

I wrote in an earlier chapter that *practice doesn't make perfect.* Marriage, like long-term investments, requires the discipline to stick it out through the ups and downs of the market, trusting that eventually it will pay off. Don't approach marriage as though you were a rookie stock-broker, tricked by every hiccup caused by fluctuating oil prices or orange juice shortages. Make a wise decision, and then stick with it for the long haul.

After all Jennie and I have been through and fought through and prayed through, out of sheer laziness I would never for a moment consider divorce. We have worked so hard to get where we are. I am committed to the blood, sweat, and tears I have in this investment, and I am bound and determined to watch it mature. Leaving her would be like selling Apple or Google stock to invest in a company that caught my attention on *Shark Tank.* I've said it before, and I'll say it again: if she ever leaves me, I'm going with her!

JESUS HAS ENTERED THE BUILDING

There is a Bible story that beautifully illustrates the kind of roll-up-your-sleeves-and-get-to-work effort that success in marriage requires:

On the third day there was a wedding in Cana of Galilee, and the mother of Jesus was there. Now both Jesus and His disciples were invited to the wedding. And when they ran out of wine, the mother of Jesus said to Him, "They have no wine."

Jesus said to her, "Woman, what does your concern have to do with Me? My hour has not yet come."

His mother said to the servants, "Whatever He says to you, do it."

Now there were set there six waterpots of stone, according to the manner of purification of the Jews, containing twenty or thirty gallons apiece. Jesus said to them, "Fill the waterpots with water." And they filled them up to the brim. And He said to them, "Draw some out now, and take it to the master of the feast." And they took it. When the master of the feast had tasted the water that was made wine, and did not know where it came from (but the servants who had drawn the water knew), the master of the feast called the bridegroom. And he said to him, "Every man at the beginning sets out the good wine, and when the guests have well drunk, then the inferior. You have kept the good wine until now!" (John 2:1–10)

I love this miracle and can't help but laugh when I read it. I like to imagine the maître d' tasted that wine and said, "Wow! I thought we were all out!" then asked his employees, "What year is this?"

"Uh, year?" they might have responded.

"Yeah, what *vintage* is it?" he would have pressed.

"Well, right now . . ."

"No, I mean, was it aged for years in oak barrels in Napa?"

"No," they would have clarified, "it was made like ten seconds ago, in the bathtub . . ."

Ridiculousness aside, this miracle is significant because it is the first miracle Jesus ever performed. Which makes a statement, doesn't it? I mean, it took thousands of years for God's Son to come to earth, fulfilling God's promise to destroy sin, conquer death, and rescue humanity. After all the prophecies and waiting for the four hundred silent years between Malachi and Matthew, he finally showed up. About time! At the age of thirty, he began his public ministry, the Holy Spirit came upon him at his baptism, and with all the power in the universe coursing through him he—wait for it—went to a wedding and solved a catering catastrophe.

What?

Talk about the world's most over-qualified bartender. This is like the president selling stamps in a post office. The fate of humanity is hanging in the balance, and Jesus is whipping up some pinot noir at a wedding reception.

Interestingly, the first item on God's agenda after creating the world in the Old Testament was also a wedding. So why shouldn't the New Testament start that way too? Relationships matter to God. If you go to the other bookend of Jesus' public ministry, you'll find him at the tomb of Lazarus, where he raises his friend from the dead. What's the message? From the altar to the grave, Jesus cares about every detail of our lives.

In case you are still not satisfied with that explanation for Jesus' presence at a party during such urgent times (and, depending on what church you attend, perhaps you are squirming a bit at his helping make an alcoholic beverage), John tells us very clearly why Jesus was there. Maybe you missed it. Look at verse 2 again: "Now both Jesus and His disciples were *invited* to the wedding" (emphasis added).

Jesus was invited. If you know only one thing about Jesus, know this: he will come into any situation where he is invited. Is he a part of *your* marriage? Did you put him on the guest list? If you feel like he isn't involved in your relationship, it's not because he doesn't want to come—he won't just party crash. You have not because you ask not (James 4:2).

GOING ALL THE WAY

Another takeaway from John 2 is that the ingredients for a miracle are always within reach. God puts to use what we have. We get stuck because we focus on what we don't have, but he wants us to utilize what we've been given.

John 2 also teaches us that miracles take faith, and obedience is necessary for blessing. Sometimes it may seem stupid or crazy— or both—to follow God. I guarantee the servants' hands shook as they ladled water from a stone pot and

> If you know only one thing about Jesus, know this: he will come into any situation where he is invited.

fed it to their boss on the authority of the mother of some-one they had just met. If I have learned anything from the journey of following God, it's that if you feel crazy, you are probably doing it right.

But to me the biggest lesson from this text is that *you can have as much as you want*.

Take a look at Jesus' instruction and the servants' obedience one more time: "Now there were set there six waterpots of stone . . . containing twenty or thirty gallons apiece. Jesus said to them, 'Fill the waterpots with water.' And *they filled them up to the brim*" (John 2:6–7, emphasis added). Those six waterpots were massive; each one held twenty to thirty gallons. The King James Version says that each one contained "two or three firkins." A firkin sounds like something Miley Cyrus would do at a party, but it is actually a unit of measurement that represented ten gallons of fluid. The point is that these pots were big, and it would have been a major undertaking to fill just one of them. Remember, the servants couldn't flip on a faucet or turn on a hose. We are talking about going out to the well, pulling up a bucket of water, carrying it to the pot, and pouring it out. To fill all six pots would have required going back again and again and again and again.

The text says they filled them "to the brim." That impresses me to no end, because the servants had no guar-antees this plan was going to work. To fill them up even halfway still would have been backbreaking work. To fill them three-fourths full—impressive. But they filled them to the brim. They didn't stop going to the well until there was no more room for water.

The guests received 120 to 180 gallons of wine, because that is how much water the servants poured in.

What does this have to do with relationships? So many people live and operate with only enough in the tank to get by. The bare minimum. Running low is a way of life; I'm thinking of the 10 percent battery life remaining on my wife's iPhone (which makes me uncomfortable) or the 10 percent gas remaining in my car (which makes my wife uncomfortable). Many people also flirt with the redline relationally. They're running on fumes, hanging on by a thread.

Living that way is cruising for a bruising, because when you put in only what is required and no more, all it takes is one bad month / one bad fight / one unforeseen crisis to push you beyond the point of no return.

Jennie and I have endured a marriage storm that, statistically speaking, should have done us in. When parents have to bury a child, the relationship often doesn't survive. And sadly, we have seen that happen to many couples. I write this with all humility, giving all glory to God: Jennie's and my marriage, while not without its issues, is better and stronger today than it's ever been.

I have a hunch that a trial, such as a child's going to heaven, doesn't destroy the marriage; it just exposes the weakness of a marriage's foundation. Going into the furnace explodes hairline fractures. The beautiful thing about trials, though, is that they only amplify and enhance what goes in; while they will make a weak marriage weaker, they make a strong marriage stronger.

This is why it's critical that you train for the trials you are not yet in. What was done during the seven years of plenty, when the crops flourished, got Joseph and Egypt through the seven years of lack, when famine struck. Skinny cows and fat cows, yo.

Barely enough is not good enough. We need to approach marriage with a to-the-brim mentality.

FEEL THE RHYTHM, FEEL THE RHYME

In our home, Thursday night is date night. I take Jennie to dinner and look her in the eyes and tell her I love her. Sometimes we just wordlessly sigh back and forth across the table. Often we go to a movie, and Jennie cries when we walk through the lobby, because the night our daughter Lenya went to heaven, they saw a matinee of *Monsters, Inc.*, and Jennie took Lenya to go potty one last time. I hold her hand and wipe the tears from her cheek as we get in the car. We laugh. We pray. We ask forgiveness and make plans. We share our dreams and fears and let each other see our souls naked and unashamed. When we were young and poor, our date nights were trips to Costco to eat a hot dog (and samples). Romance can happen on any budget.

Date night is sacred and replenishing. At different phases, each of our kids have cried when we left them with the babysitter. It's okay. I think it's good for them to see me love and dote on their mom, because it sets the bar high for the men in their future lives to measure up to. They don't cry when I take them on daddy-daughter dates. In addition to these Thursdays, Jennie and I also take getaways together each year. We make these deposits into our relationship account faithfully, whether or not we feel like we "need" it any given week. We don't want to bounce relational checks, so we work hard to keep more than is needed in the accounts. Scraping by paycheck-to-paycheck is not our goal; margin is. We want relational reserves.

You will be able to pull wine out of your marriage to the extent that you pour water into it. God can't bless what you don't offer him. Sow sparingly, reap sparingly. If you keep your stone pots from running low, God will turn that water into merlot. And trust me when I say this: if you don't date your mate, the devil will find someone who will. No one can stop you from having a marriage that's incredible; you just have to fill your pots to the brim with the water of love, generosity, forgiveness, time, affection, communication, and intimacy.

GIVE MOSES A PINK SLIP

Jesus' first miracle is eerily reminiscent of Moses' first miracle. When Moses told Pharaoh to release the Israelites from slavery and Pharoah said no, Moses turned the Nile River into blood.

Interesting. In Moses you have a picture of Jesus. A preview of coming attractions. Moses knew this. He said, "The Lord will raise up a prophet like me from your midst. You should listen to him" (Deuteronomy 18:15, author's paraphrase). The law came through Moses, but grace and truth came through Jesus Christ. Moses was meant to lead us to Jesus, to be a placeholder until Jesus arrived.

If your relationship isn't working, is it because you're letting Moses run the show—eye for an eye, tit for tat, tooth for tooth? You bought this, so I can spend that. I watched the kids last week, so it's your turn. You aren't pleasing me. He doesn't respect me, so I won't submit. She cut me off sexually, so I cut her off from affection. All that leads to is a bloody mess.

If you both allow Jesus to be in charge in your souls and in your relationship, he will lead you to a new and better way. He will not turn water to blood; he'll turn water to wine. You'll be able to enjoy and savor your life because of a little thing called grace, in which you each look at the other through the lens of the cross. When you're no longer earning your standing or constantly keeping score, you can freely forgive because you are forgiven.

Maybe, in your relationship, you need to give Moses a pink slip and let him know Jesus is taking the wheel. And if you've never given your heart to Jesus, I pray that today would be the day, that even as you close this chapter you would surrender to him. He died for you, he rose from the dead, and if you call out to him in faith, he will save you from your sins.

> There is no way you can be right with your mate until you get right with your Maker.

Maybe you don't have a marriage problem. It might be you have a *soul* problem. Give your heart to Jesus, and walk in relationship with him. There is no way you can be right with your mate until you get right with your Maker.

CHAPTER 11

Breaking the Fourth Wall

The mustached man grabbed my arm roughly and said, "Come with me." Anger flashed in his eyes. As he led me forcefully to the front of the store, he explained that he was part of the undercover security team, and he had witnessed me shoplifting.

This was a revelation to me. I was shopping for a few last-minute items before leaving for a mission trip to Nepal, and besides the few toiletries in my basket, I hadn't touched anything else in the store. However, his aggression was so convincing that I almost doubted my own innocence. This guy had clearly missed his calling as a DEA task force assassin ninja warlord commander. (Why is there always an inverse correlation between someone's level of authority and how seriously they take themselves?)

He took me to an office, where he thoroughly inspected the few items I had in the basket and made me empty my pockets before concluding that I had not been shoplifting after all. With a sheepish look and a perfunctory apology, he reluctantly released me into the general population.

The impact that experience had on me was immediate and twofold: First, I was cured of the desire to ever return to that particular store and will go out of my way to find an alternative. On the rare occasions I have had no choice but to return, I've done so begrudgingly, and subsequent visits have done little to unsully the brand for me. The second and more interesting effect has been the greater awareness of the fact that I am always being watched, and not just by closed-circuit security cameras. I never knew that there were plainclothes "civilians" involved in loss prevention. It both makes sense and is creepy, and it's led to a distrust of other shoppers when I am in retail spaces. I'll see someone picking out jeans at Costco or acting interested in a blender at Williams-Sonoma and think, *That's so fake.* Then I pretend like I am going to shove a waffle maker into my jacket, just to see if they'll twitch.

THROW THE BABY IN THE RIVER

There was a day when one of the most significant figures in all of history thought he was in the clear, but in fact he was being watched. It's our main man Moses, whom we talked about a little bit in the previous chapter. Any larger-than-life character's origin story is compelling, and Moses' does not disappoint. He was an Israelite born in Egypt when they were slaves under the reign of Pharaoh. The descendants of Jacob had originally sought sanctuary in Egypt when Joseph, one of their own, was the second in command. But Joseph had long since died, and the Israelites had become enslaved. Now several million strong, they were seen as a threat to the Egyptians. So Pharaoh hatched a plan to wipe them out.

Since they were reproducing so quickly, Pharaoh instructed the midwives, who were all in his employ, to kill every Israelite boy at birth. When the midwives chose to ignore those orders, he issued an edict that all newborn males must be thrown into the Nile River alive. The result of this horrible decision would be that only Israelite women would remain, and they would be forced to intermarry with the Egyptians. Soon there would be no children of Israel left at all.

Many, many baby boys died barbaric deaths as they were torn from their screaming, tearful parents' arms and thrown into the crocodile-infested waters. Today in America one out of five pregnancies ends in abortion.[1] So many lives are senselessly cut short before ever getting to experience life outside of the womb.

We experienced firsthand the nonchalant nature in which abortions are routinely and clinically suggested when Jennie was pregnant with our first daughter. We planned to wait five years before having kids, but we'd been married less than a year when Jennie found out we were expecting. This was in the days before Pinterest and a proliferation of cute ways to break the news—she simply called me and told me on the phone. (I would not recommend that. I was in between meetings at work and almost fell over.)

We made an appointment with our physician to confirm the pregnancy. After Jennie's blood was drawn, the doctor finally came in. He was a weasely little dude, with glasses on the bridge of his nose and a big mustache. (I know, I keep bringing up mustaches, but I honestly have nothing against them. If you have one, I'm totally cool with that. I'm just saying, his was pretty outrageous.) He came into the room, looked at the papers in his hand, and without even really looking at us said, "Yup. Yup. You're pregnant."

We were totally stunned, just sitting there absorbing this news, and he continued, "What do you want to do about it?"

We looked at each other, having no clue how to respond. I was thinking, *I guess we need to get a crib. Diapers. A Baby Bjorn. I have no idea how to install a car seat. My head is spinning. We're not prepared for this.*

When our response indicated how out of our depth we felt taking the plunge of parenthood, he interjected, his voice full of surprise, "Wait. You're going to keep it?"

It was then that we realized what he had actually been asking us. "What do you want to do about it?" was code for "Would you like me to terminate that pregnancy for you? Would you like me to just get rid of it?"

It was kind of like when you are at a restaurant, and you have only a tiny bit left on your plate, and you haven't touched it for a while, and the waitress comes over to say, "Are you done with that, hon? Do you want me to get that out of your way, sugar?"

If you are done eating, you'd be like, "Oh, yeah. Just get that out of the way."

That's how easy in that moment it would have been to say, "Yeah, just get rid of it. It wasn't a part of our plan, so no, we don't want to keep it." He made it so easy and nonchalant with his question.

I spoke up, "Uh, yeah. We'll definitely be keeping *it*."

At that point, he looked at us for the first time. Taking off his glasses, he said, "You know what? I think you two are going to make really great parents."

Apparently the bar is really, really low. All you have to do is not kill your baby when you find out about it, and you are in the running for mother and father of the year.

I realize not every parent is ready to have a kid, and not every single woman who gets pregnant is in a place in life where it would be the best thing for her to raise a child, but there are tons of people all over the place who would love to raise your baby, even if you can't. So if you ever find yourself pregnant but not wanting to keep it yourself, please don't throw it into the river. There are people champing at the bit to have a child in their lives.

I'm not a guy who pickets Planned Parenthood facilities. But when I think about the statistics on abortion, all I can think about is what the world would be like without my daughter Alivia, who, while I write this chapter, is playing in the sand on the beach in Waikiki while with me on a preaching trip to Honolulu. We got up at 5:30 a.m. to get a jumpstart on the day and watched the sunrise together on a bench. Yesterday we rented boards and paddled out into the world-famous surf. She is ten years old and so strong and mature and wise beyond her years.

Moses' parents weren't willing to part with him either. They didn't see just a baby when they looked at him. The Bible says that when Amram and Jochebed looked into his face, they saw that he was no ordinary child (Hebrews 11:23). The truth is that there is no such thing as an ordinary child. Every single person has value and a calling on his or her life. Guided by this conviction, by faith, they disobeyed Pharaoh's command and hid Moses rather than tossing him into the river. Eventually his crying got too loud and so they resorted to floating him down the river in a little ark. Pharaoh's daughter found him and adopted him as her son.

I find it fascinating that Moses' life was spared through the river, because that same river was supposed to kill him. The worst thing you endured should have killed you, but now God is going to use that pain to release power in your life. The devil might have meant it for evil, but God will use it for good. And not just for you but for those who are blessed through you.

> I find it fascinating that Moses' life was spared through the river, because that same river was supposed to kill him.

Jesus' life shows the same thing. The devil thought he had won as Jesus hung on the cross. But little did Satan know that the cross was actually an offensive weapon and would be his undoing. In God's hands, what is meant to destroy you can become a source of rescue!

The best part of Moses' story is that right after Pharaoh's daughter claimed him, his older sister, Miriam, who had been trailing the basket as a spotter, jumped out of the bushes and offered to find a wet nurse for him. Pharaoh's daughter loved the idea, and, of course, Miriam knew just the person. So Moses' mom, Jochebed, ended up getting paid to raise her son until he was kindergarten-age by the man who wanted Moses dead in the first place. Don't tell me God doesn't have a sense of humor!

During those few precious years with her son, it is clear that Moses' mother whispered his true identity to him and made it her aim to tuck promises into her son's heart. Eventually these truths took hold and bloomed inside his spirit. Though he was raised in the palace and slept on Egyptian cotton, he couldn't shake the thought that he was meant to live for more.

THE RIGHT THING
THE WRONG WAY

One day Moses happened to witness an Egyptian taskmaster beating a Hebrew slave. Out of solidarity with the Hebrew, whom he knew deep down shared his blood, he beat the Egyptian to death and hid his body in the sand. The details of the account of this crime of passion are vitally important to what I want you to understand, so read it carefully: "So he looked this way and that way, and when he saw no one, he killed the Egyptian and hid him in the sand" (Exodus 2:12).

Did you catch that? This outburst of wrath (which, by the way, would cost him forty years of his life) came about because he looked "this way" (to the left) and "that way" (to the right), and seeing no one, he falsely believed that the coast was clear. What he failed to do is what you and I often forget to do: he never looked up. Giving no thought to what heaven would think about his actions, he took matters into his own hands. He did the right thing (helping a fellow Israelite) in the wrong way (murdering a random taskmaster) and made a mess of things.

There is much to be learned from Moses' mistake. When you live life looking only left and right you create problems. There is incredible power that comes from looking up and acknowledging the presence of God. That is why it is essential that you learn how to break the fourth wall in your life.

BREAKING CHARACTER

The fourth wall is a term from the world of theater, cinema, and literature that refers to the invisible wall that separates the audience from the characters in the play, movie, or novel. The characters are supposed to pretend we are not watching them or reading about them as they go about their business. If you have ever seen a movie set, the rooms are usually missing a wall where the camera goes. In a theater, that opening in the set is where the audience sits. (Watching a movie is kind of a weird voyeuristic thing, if you think about it. We pay money to watch people sitting in a fake environment, pretending they are people they are not and acting like no one is watching them go about their business.)

When an actor or performer directly acknowledges the audience or looks into the camera, it is referred to as "breaking the fourth wall." For example, when Peter Pan asks the children watching the movie to clap their hands to save Tinkerbell's life, he is breaking the fourth wall. When Jim on *The Office* smirks into the camera after Michael or

Dwight do something crazy, or when Ferris Bueller talks to us through the camera, narrating his own movie, they are breaking the fourth wall.

This trick is used by directors to shake things up, to pull the audience into the story, or to break the awkwardness of a scene. Sometimes it is amusing; other times it is just plain chilling. (I'm talking to you, Kevin Spacey.)

At its essence, to break the fourth wall is to stop pretending that you are by yourself, to admit you are being watched, and to acknowledge your audience.

Your goal in life should be to do exactly that: to channel your inner Ronald Reagan and "tear down this wall," ending the false separation between yourself and God and embracing the fact that everything we do, every line we say, is being watched. There is in fact an eye in the sky. Listen to how Solomon described it: "The eyes of the LORD are in every place, / Keeping watch on the evil and the good" (Proverbs 15:3).

The Duke of Wellington once noted that Napoleon Bonaparte's presence on the field made the difference of forty thousand men.[2] His soldiers fought differently when their leader was with them. Your life will take on and tap into new meaning, significance, and strength to the degree that you learn to look into the camera and acknowledge God's presence in your life.

SMILE—YOU'RE ON CAMERA!

There was a day when David—shepherd, warrior, poet, and king of Israel—had his own personal *Truman Show* moment. Like Jim Carrey's character, David realized that everything he did was being watched. The psalm he wrote to describe the experience is both one of the most powerful declarations of the continual reality of God's presence and one of the most clear-cut decimations of the fourth wall anywhere in the Bible.

> O LORD, You have searched me and known me.
> You know my sitting down and my rising up;
> You understand my thought afar off.
> You comprehend my path and my lying down,
> And are acquainted with all my ways.
> For there is not a word on my tongue,
> But behold, O LORD, You know it altogether.
> You have hedged me behind and before,
> And laid Your hand upon me.
> Such knowledge is too wonderful for me;
> It is high, I cannot attain it.
>
> Where can I go from Your Spirit?
> Or where can I flee from Your presence?
> If I ascend into heaven, You are there;
> If I make my bed in hell, behold, You are there.
> If I take the wings of the morning,
> And dwell in the uttermost parts of the sea,
> Even there Your hand shall lead me,
> And Your right hand shall hold me.
> If I say, "Surely the darkness shall fall on me,"
> Even the night shall be light about me;
> Indeed, the darkness shall not hide from You,

But the night shines as the day;
The darkness and the light are both alike to You.
    (Psalm 139:1–12)

There are two theological terms we need to understand to break through the fourth wall: God's *omnipresence* and his *manifest presence*.

Let's talk briefly about omnipresence first. (I say *briefly* because any longer than that and I will get a migraine.) Omnipresence is one of God's attributes. The word literally means that he is in all places at all times. Or to put it another way, wherever you are, there he is. That's why David wrote, "If I ascend into heaven . . . If I take the wings of the morning, / And dwell in the uttermost parts of the sea"—check, check, check: God is there (vv. 8–9). But—this is where it gets really mind-blowing—just as God is where you are going to be, he is also still where you just were. God isn't just one step ahead of you, beating you there; he is also still where you aren't while simultaneously being where you are presently. (See what I mean about the headache?) David had the same reaction: "Such knowledge is too wonderful for me; / It is high, I cannot attain it" (v. 6). In other words, thinking about God's omnipresence caused David to reach for the Excedrin.

But it's true.

Just ask Jonah, who tried to "flee . . . from the presence of the LORD" (Jonah 1:3) and found out the hard way that God is the worst person in the world to play hide-and-seek with. Like it or not, there is absolutely nothing you can do about this fact. You have never not been with God. Not for one second have you been alone. Last week and early this morning, and during worship on Sunday, and Friday night at midnight, and on prom night in high school, and when you did your taxes, and that time you yelled at your wife, and when the clerk at the grocery store gave you too much change, and when you were super kind to that stranger—at your best and at your worst, God is always with you, even to the end of time: "For the ways of man are before the eyes of the LORD, / And He ponders all his paths" (Proverbs 5:21).

Whether thinking about God's omnipresence fills your heart with courage or covers you with shame has everything to do with who you think God is. If you think God is vengeful and angry, then the doctrine I am preaching makes you live in fear, because he is watching you like Santa Claus and you imagine he can't wait until you blow it so he can stick coal in your stocking.

If this is how you feel, then you not only misunderstand God's nature and heart but also his knowledge of the future.

Instead, consider this: God is loving and kind. A good God. He is for you, not against you. He wants to bless you! If you doubt that, just take a quick trip to the cross, where he was willing to give the most precious gift that has ever been given in order to save your life.

And—news flash!—God knows the end from the beginning. He has never been surprised. Pastor Robert Morris wrote, "Nothing has ever occurred to God."[3] He has all knowledge and exists outside of time, so he sees the end from the beginning. That means he already knows what you are going to do and isn't hoping you blow it. He knew your worst mistakes before you made them—and loved you anyway. Because he has chosen to give you free will, and he won't tamper with your decisions, he is cheering you on when you choose to do right and is willing to give you grace when you choose to do wrong. We see this image of God vividly in 2 Chronicles 16:9: "For the eyes of the LORD run to and fro throughout the whole earth, to show Himself strong on behalf of those whose heart is loyal to Him."

The purpose of God's surveillance is strength and support. He watches so he can back you up, not so he can build a case and then blackmail you or bust you like an overzealous security guard. Your God wants to reward your victories, not rub your nose in your failures. If you properly understand omnipresence, the result will be increased power, not paranoia. You won't refuse to shop online or go all Joaquin Phoenix and wear an aluminum-foil hat. Instead, you'll raise your hands to the heavens in praise because you have backup!

Does an undercover agent feel scared that she is being watched by the intelligence officers in the van across the street, or dread the fact that there is a SWAT team on standby ready to deploy if she speaks the emergency phrase into her wire? Of course not. She understands that the reason she's being watched is for her safety and support. And so will you, when you dismantle the fourth wall you have been hiding behind and, like Jacob, say: "Surely the LORD is in this place, and I did not know it" (Genesis 28:16).

Now that you have a basic idea of what omnipresence is, let's talk about manifest presence. Manifest presence is when the God who is always with you comes closer to you. I don't presume to understand this, but the Bible teaches that the same God who is in every place can somehow come closer.

The LORD is near to those who have a broken heart,
And saves such as have a contrite spirit. (Psalm 34:18)

The LORD is near to all who call upon Him,
To all who call upon Him in truth. (Psalm 145:18)

"The LORD your God in your midst,
The Mighty One, will save;
He will rejoice over you with gladness,
He will quiet you with His love,
He will rejoice over you with singing." (Zephaniah 3:17)

I haven't a clue how this works, but it's true. I've felt it. Never have I sensed God lean so close to me as when my heart hurt the worst. And no matter what I am going through, when I call on God's name, I feel him flooding into my soul again. This is the manifest presence of God, and it is available to you anytime you want. Scripture invites us not to stop at merely being constantly with God, but to take the relationship to another level by experiencing and benefiting from his presence.

We see God's manifest presence even before the fall. God was with Adam and Eve at all times, yet he would specifically come close and walk with them. They would hear the sound of God walking; then they would go meet him and walk with him.

When the serpent deceived them, Adam and Eve put up the first fourth wall in history by living as though God couldn't see them: eating the forbidden fruit, covering themselves in fig leaves, and hiding themselves among the trees of the garden.

And God went along with it: "Then the LORD God called

to Adam and said to him, 'Where are you?'" (Genesis 3:9). God did this not because he couldn't see them but as an invitation for them to stop running and hiding. God was still with them *geographically*, but not near them *relationally*, as he had been.

The sum of the matter is this: there is nothing you can do about being present with God, but it is up to you whether you benefit from his presence. A. W. Tozer wrote, "The presence and the manifestation of the presence are not the same. There can be the one without the other. God is here when we are wholly unaware of it. He is *manifest* only when and as we are aware of His presence."[4]

RECOGNITION LEADS TO IGNITION

When you acknowledge God's presence, you turn the key in your spiritual ignition. His presence is a benefit only if you remember it, cultivate it, and lean into it. One of the most repeated commands in Scripture is "Remember," because it is so easy to forget. Whisper to God each morning, "I know that you are here. I know you are with me." Say it when you are afraid or tempted. Say it when you are angry or disappointed. Let it become your release valve when you are ashamed. Run *to* him, not *from* him. Memory will help alter your story.

There is no limit to where you can take this, because God will fill whatever space you create. God said, "Those who seek me find me" (Proverbs 8:17 NIV). Like the ocean that floods into the hole on the beach you dug between tides, he will fill whatever you open up and make available. I mentioned earlier that we check our phones on average one hundred and fifty times a day, which breaks down to once every six minutes. You probably just did it, didn't you? Busted. (That's why mine is in the other room, and the computer I am typing this on is in "Do Not Disturb" mode. I don't trust myself, and I can't wait to get to the next chapter. I saved the best for last!) What if you got into the regular habit of looking up? How good would it be for your heart if one hundred and fifty times a day you acknowledged God's presence and smiled at him in your soul? What if you invited him into your life at work or at school and gave him a seat at the table in your hobbies and finances, even in your loneliness?

I came across an old hymn by Oliver Holden that will give you a brand-new way of looking at what is all around you:

> They who seek the throne of grace,
> Find that throne in every place;
> If we live a life of prayer,
> God is present everywhere.
>
> In our sickness or our health,
> In our want or in our wealth,
> If we look to God in prayer,
> God is present everywhere.[5]

Interestingly enough, even though God is omnipresent, there is one place he won't invade unless invited—the human heart: "Behold, I stand at the door and knock. If anyone hears My voice and opens the door, I will come in to him and dine with him, and he with Me" (Revelation 3:20). To benefit from God's touch inside your spirit, you must welcome him in.

As you seek to rise up and live a life of strength and honor, nothing will give you greater peace and authority than embracing the power that comes from practicing the presence of God. We live in a world where people only look to the right and to the left. If you want to swipe right, you must look up. Had Moses looked up, he wouldn't have killed the Egyptian, which cost him so much in the long run. God did want Moses to get the Israelites out of Egypt, but not by killing one random soldier; instead Moses was to stroll into Pharaoh's throne room and calmly ask for them to be released. And instead of pathetically burying one man in the sand, he would raise his staff, buoyed by God's strength, and all of Pharaoh's troops would be buried under the Red Sea. Timing is everything.

Even if, like Moses, you zigged when you should have zagged, God is still with you and still wants to draw near to you. His presence is not based on your performance. He's not *only* with you on your good days or *more* with you on your good days. He is *always* with you, because that's who he is, not because of anything you have or haven't done. I don't care what skeletons are in your closet: whether you were once on drugs, whether you've spent time behind bars, or whether your marriage failed. The things behind you are no match for the one who is with you.

How do you begin to move forward from a mess you have made?

His presence is not based on your performance.

Let your identity come from the way God has rescued you and not with what you needed rescuing from in the first place. We can romanticize the story, but the truth is Moses had a turbulent upbringing. Things were so stacked against him when he was born that the safest thing his parents could do was put him in a tiny boat and set him floating down a river full of crocodiles. He had to pretend his mom was his babysitter; then once he was weaned, he grew up in the court of the man who had tried to kill him. The deranged Hitler character became his grandpa. Sounds like an expensive therapy bill to me.

God brought good out of Moses' challenges in the end. But when you are in the thick of it, it can be hard to see that. Moses could have ended up a very confused, very mixed-up puppy. But note that the name Moses, which means "drawn out," was given to him because he was saved from the river, not because he was cast into it. His name came from his deliverance.

This is key for you and me. It's so easy to get stuck, to fixate on the bad things you have been through. To focus on the hurt—that you weren't loved, or that you are divorced, or that you are an addict, or that you are fatherless, or that you were sexually abused.

If you're not careful, this bitterness can turn into a victim mentality and a wounded spirit. You can let it control you and give you your name. It's easy to be defined by your dysfunction, but it's not necessary.

Just as Moses means "drawn out," you have been called

out. The Greek word translated as *church* in the New Testament literally means "called out" ones. Jesus loved you so much that he called you out of the crocodile-infested darkness into his marvelous light. Royal blood was shed for you! You have been rescued.

A *60 Minutes* special called "The Recyclers: From Trash Comes Triumph" once brought me to tears.[6] I saw the episode on my iPad in bed one night and just the subtitle made me sit up straight against the headboard and lean in.

It was about a place I had never heard about called Cateura, a town built on a garbage dump in Paraguay. Twenty-five hundred families live there in the midst of the garbage. Twelve tons of trash is brought to the dump every day. The townspeople comb through the trash around the clock, constantly on the lookout for whatever they can salvage and sell. The quality of life is unimaginable.

But Don Colé Gomez figured out how to make instruments from the trash he lived in. He turned oven trays and oil barrels into violins and cellos, completed with recycled strings. Drain pipes, coins, and bottle caps came together to form saxophones and trumpets, and dessert tins formed the bodies of guitars.

His creations enabled the school in Cateura to open a music program. Families there never could have afforded real instruments; a real violin would be worth more than a home. The program opened up new possibilities for many children—most of whom would have ended up in gangs otherwise. The symphony has toured the country and the world and was featured in a documentary made about the program called *Landfill Harmonic*.

My heart was racing by the time the story was over. That is our God! He makes music out of what the world throws away. From trash comes triumph!

He takes the garbage life hands us and redeems it, turns it into gold.

Beauty from ashes.

Light from dark places.

He makes all things work together for good.

Every day you have a choice: you can dwell on the fact that you were put into hardship, or you can focus on and rejoice over the fact that God drew you out. God wants to bring you to a place where you are not defined by your dysfunction but by your deliverance. It's easy to be so shaken and scarred by your trials that, even though they're behind you, you still smell of them, and all you can think about is how hard life has been. I believe not only that you will not be consumed by the fires you have been through, but that you won't even smell like smoke. At this very moment, as you read these words, God's Spirit wants to heal your wounded spirit and free you from a victim's mentality. His desire is for you to see that you are more than a conqueror, and he is leading you in victory.

You are not defined by your dysfunction but by your deliverance.

I dare you to raise your palms to the ceiling and whisper to him, "I am willing." In God's economy it doesn't matter where you begin but whose hands you are in. He loves nothing more than doing wonderful things with broken beings.

Winter Is Coming

Jennie and I were walking down the streets of SoHo in New York. If you have read *Through the Eyes of a Lion*, this was the same trip when we attended *Spiderman: Turn Off the Dark* and I began writing a message that would be the most difficult and decisive I have given as a pastor. Between writing the sermon and delivering it, my family experienced a loss that had previously been only in our nightmares. The message I wrote was about God's power over darkness—but then we went from the lecture to the lab and found the strength I was preaching about. It's one thing to proclaim Jesus' power over death in the sunshine, but I found great strength waiting for me when I clung to it in the shadows. Preaching only days after burying our child was an act of defiance: we ran toward the roar and discovered the way God can turn impossible pain into incredible power.

While we were in the city, Jennie and I popped into a little store that caught her eye. Inside we discovered that the store sold children's jewelry. I immediately thought of Alivia and Lenya (ages seven and five at the time) and the fact that

I had been wanting to give them rings to wear on their ring fingers as a reminder of our ongoing conversation about relationships and romance, strength and honor. When she was in fifth grade (at precisely the same time I was being introduced to pornography), Jennie had been given a key at a church event in San Jose, California, and was told to save it and herself for her husband one day. It wasn't easy, but without knowing my name she fought for me; on our wedding night she handed me the key, and with it she gave herself. These rings for our girls were our way of continuing that beautiful heritage.

The night before, the enormous Christmas tree at Rockefeller Center had been turned on. The trappings of Christmas were everywhere, so even though part of me wanted to give the girls their rings as soon as we got home, we decided to wait for Christmas day.

When we got home, we cut down a Christmas tree in the woods, as had been our tradition since moving to Montana. It's one of our most painful family traditions for me, because I am allergic to Christmas trees. I break out in hives if one branch so much as touches my skin. This complicates my job as chief lighting engineer. But if I wear gloves and a long-sleeved shirt, and sometimes a hoodie, I manage to get by with only minor itchiness. After I put the lights up, Jennie and the girls hang the ornaments.

The night we decorated, Lenya was wearing a red Santa hat. Since I had gloves on, she thoughtfully kept bringing me handfuls of popcorn and allowing me to eat them out of her hand—while pretending to be a deranged reindeer—as she giggled. (Dad life forever, yo.) The rings were wrapped with all the other little gifts we had bought for our four little arrows. There weren't as many gifts as usual, because the day after Christmas all six of us were scheduled to fly to California for their main present—a day at Disneyland.

Life doesn't always go as planned. Sometimes things go off the rails. Someone said that plans never survive first contact with the enemy. Mike Tyson quipped, "Everybody has a plan until they get punched in the mouth."[1] Sometimes life doesn't cooperate. Jennie and I bought those rings with smiles in our hearts and joy all over our faces. They represented a mission I took more seriously than Frodo's quest to reach the volcano.

I couldn't wait to see Alivia and Lenya open them and wear them. It gave me so much happiness to think of pulling the girls close to me and telling them how special they are and how it is an enormous honor, as the man in their life, to protect and love them as princesses. I planned to kiss their foreheads and tell them, as I often did, that God would one day bring each of them a man who would love and serve them the way they have seen me treat them and their mother, and not to give themselves to anyone before then. Our message to them was not to settle but to hold out for honor. The rings themselves weren't very expensive, because we knew they would be lost, and they would be replaced as many times as necessary. This would be an ongoing conversation, not a single talk. A relationship, not a chastity belt.

Lenya went home to heaven while the rings were still unopened. She left this world with her daddy's breath in her lungs and her mom's prayers in her ears as we did CPR and begged God for more time with her here on earth. Five days before we planned to give these gifts, she was gone. The sadness that detonated that night was followed by countless smaller explosions, as we stepped on unexpected emotional landmines that triggered new grief over our realization that a million moments had been pried from our fingers.

Our shoulders shook with grief as we wept upon the discovery of the rings. Death had snatched from us a memory still uncreated, but the anticipation of its arrival had already produced happiness and warmth. Having it plucked from our hearts without being lived was icy and mean. It hurt and felt wasteful. Regret over waiting, mixed with anger at what had been taken, left me helplessly spinning my tires, unable to do anything with such powerful feelings.

Anything you do while you are grieving is like screaming under water: the dreadful feeling that no one can hear you and that nothing you do can change anything puts a very heavy weight on your chest and fills you inexplicably with adrenaline that could help you sprint but makes sitting still very hard.

Fortunately, in the raging storm of sadness, the rainbow of God's overpowering love would intermittently light up the sky. Dazzling multicolored ribbons of light waves exploding from heaven to earth never come on cloudless days. They are impossible without the same wind and moisture that causes darkness and gloom. The same raindrops falling from the sky become prisms for the rays of light to reveal their true colors. Rainbows are always around us— they are just invisible without sadness in the sky. The same nerve endings that allow you to feel the pain of searing loss also allow you to feel God's presence and his glory to a degree that previously could not have been reached. When you don't numb the hurt but rather grit your teeth and face it, God meets you there and allows the deep trough of your sorrow to become a reservoir full of his presence. As Jesus said, "Blessed are those who mourn" (Matthew 5:4).

The Comforter whispered to my heart that we weren't only to weep that we hadn't been able to give Lenya her ring during her life. We were to entrust it to her even in death, believing that the grave couldn't and wouldn't stop our love. Jesus' life and power has overcome the last enemy's attempts to rob me of my right as her father. Defiance filled my chest, and my jaw stiffened. I told Jennie my plan, and we unwrapped Lenya's ring and brought it with us to the funeral home on the day of her burial, the day after Christmas.

Lenya's lifeless body lying in that small, white box made my knees shake, but I felt God grab my heart like a cat picks up a kitten in danger—by the scruff of its neck. (It's the same way I would grab the shoulders of Alivia's snowboarding jacket as we got off the chairlift when she was learning to snowboard.) I felt God forcefully putting into my heart words that came out of my mouth in that moment.

"That's not her. She's with Jesus.

"This body was once her home, and once it is transformed in the resurrection on the last day, it will be her home again, but presently, as it is, this is not her."

With a peace I wasn't expecting, we enjoyed tender and special moments with this body we enjoyed seeing her in for five beautiful years. This was the body that we saw on the ultrasound in Jennie's womb. The one I scooped up in my arms and twirled around and around in circles. Our Lenya

Lion. Jennie handed me the ring, and when it was on the ring finger of her left hand, I stroked her hair and sobbed.

Before a tree is a tree, it is an acorn. An entire building springs out of a simple blueprint. World-changing inventions leap off of sketches hastily scribbled on napkins. Victory comes to those who can see past the seed. Harvests look nothing like the kernel that produced them.

> Victory comes to those who can see past the seed.

I believe in the resurrection of the dead.

Jesus rose, and one day when he returns, all those who sleep in Christ will rise bodily. We committed Lenya's body to the soil from which it came, believing it will spring forth when the trumpet sounds. It is this which anchors my soul when I stand in the cemetery and lift my eyes to the sky.

In a larger sense, that ring on her finger drives me as I write this book for you.

Death might have deprived me of the opportunity to continue the conversation with Lenya, but God will have the last laugh, because that motivates me to have it with you. What the thief has taken must be restored sevenfold. I am the father of a daughter cut down in the spring of her life, and I will have vengeance in this life and the next.

Anyone can count the seeds in an apple, but only God knows the number of apples in a single seed.[2] It is ordinarily the job of children to think of their parents' legacy. God has given Jennie and me the bittersweet honor of stewarding the legacy of our child. I believe that ring buried with Lenya's body and the conversations stolen from us are a seed. I seek to speak up as a father, for the Father, to any one of his children who will listen. This book is my message in a bottle, containing what I would have told Lenya, opened up for you.

And the message I have for you is this: hold out for honor.

You are worth more than you know. You are created in the image of God, and your value exceeds that of rubies or diamonds. You are loved, and you are lovely. You are appointed and anointed to rule and reign with God as royalty. You are the head and not the tail; you are from above and not beneath. You are a leader, not a follower. Don't rush, don't hurry, and don't settle! Enjoy your sex drive, but don't let sex drive. Let God prepare you, and believe that he is also preparing someone for you: a person after God's own heart who is passionately in love with Jesus and will honor and serve you and obey God in how he or she handles you. Learn to derive delight from God, and things you wouldn't dare to dream will come to pass in your life. No matter what is behind you, from this day forward, embrace God's plans for you.

> **Hold out for honor.**

THE REAL PRINCE CHARMING

On each of our daughters' birthdays, Jennie picks out some verses from the book of Proverbs that corresponds to her age and prays a prayer over her new year. This is part of Jennie's prayer that she wrote down in her journal when Lenya turned five, three months before her death:

I pray this year would mark a year of growth in her response to you. I pray that she would experience you at a young age and that she would want to live for you passionately. I pray as she is strong and sassy and bold and loud that these very things would be used for your glory and to make Jesus famous.

Later in the entry, she wrote:

I pray for her future husband, that he would love you more than anything and honor and respect and love her. Pray even now that he would be being raised in your house, knowing you. I pray that you would protect her purity even now. I pray that her heart would be on fire for you and set on eternity. I pray she'd be a world changer.

At the celebration of life we held for Lenya, Jennie read from that journal entry. Through tears, she told the attendees that she realized that her prayer was actually for Jesus, as Lenya is the bride of Christ, experiencing God like never before. No, she didn't get to walk an aisle at a wedding on earth, but she will get to wear white at the marriage supper of the Lamb—the ultimate party—and if you are a Christian, so will you. In a larger sense, your relationship with Jesus should help you make sense of your relationships here on earth.

Like Jennie's words and prayers that she speaks over our daughters' lives, Proverbs 31 is a letter from a mother to her son, telling him what kind of a woman to look for in a wife. She tells him not to be fooled by outward appearance, to not be tricked by a profile pic or eHarmony page. Charm is deceitful, and beauty is fleeting. She urges him not to marry someone who will be just a hot wife but also an epic mom and an awesome grandma. She tells him to pick someone he wants to get old and ugly and die with—not just a person who will look good on Instagram before she starts decomposing, but a woman who will be faithful in good times and bad, for better and worse, in sickness and health. A spouse who will take care of him if he ended up in a wheelchair, or lost his vision, or was burned in a fire, or lost his job. Solomon's mom warned him: if you choose carefully you will have a wife who isn't just a beautiful wife but a person who makes for a beautiful life.

DO NOT FEAR THE SNOW

Tucked within this epic description of the kind of a woman a godly young man should be looking for is a statement about her that has application outside of the selection of a spouse: "She is not afraid of snow for her household, for all her household is clothed with scarlet" (Proverbs 31:21).

In the ancient world, if you didn't prepare for winter, you wouldn't survive it. They didn't have electric heaters, warm cars, snowplows, or thermal underwear. Food had to be stockpiled, fuel accumulated, and warm clothing prepared. It's key that this woman was not afraid of winter, because her family was ready. She had taken the necessary steps to prepare, so she didn't have to worry about it. Life lesson: you don't have to be afraid of what you are prepared for.

Winter is not just a season; it is also a symbol that represents the end of the year, the conclusion of a cycle. Shakespeare used it this way in his play *Richard III*: "Now is the winter of our discontent / Made glorious summer by this son of York."[3]

You can look at the stages of life through a year: spring is youth, summer is the prime of life, fall is middle age, and winter is death—the end. The truth is, we are all moving slowly from youth to death: "My time is short—what's left of my life races off too fast for me to even glimpse the good. My life is going fast, like a ship under full sail, like an eagle plummeting to its prey" (Job 9:25–26 THE MESSAGE). Life is short, and only in Christ are you safe.

The color scarlet is deeply symbolic as well. Red reminds us of blood and of the dynamic picture of the salvation found in Jesus. The Bible declares that there can be no forgiveness of sin without the shedding of blood.

There is nothing you can do about winter approaching. As the narrator says in *Fight Club*, "On a long enough time line, the survival rate for everyone drops to zero."[4] But if you are clothed in scarlet, you don't need to be terrified of winter. You don't have to be scared of what you are prepared for. As Rahab did, keep the scarlet cord tied up in your window, and you won't have to fear the collapse of the city. Live under the safety and the protection of the crimson blood of Jesus. Remain in him, and walk in him.

A piece of oft-given advice is, "Don't forget where you came from." In other words, stay grounded. Dance with those who brought you. Don't get too big for your britches. I certainly agree with that, but it is also incredibly important to remember where you are going. In many ways your future is much more important than your past. You are headed to heaven, and knowledge of your destination is one of the most powerful weapons you have in your arsenal against temptation.

Read what Peter said:

> Beloved, I beg you as sojourners and pilgrims, abstain from fleshly lusts which war against the soul, having your conduct honorable among the Gentiles, that when they speak against you as evildoers, they may, by your good works which they observe, glorify God in the day of visitation. (1 Peter 2:11–12)

In these verses Peter connected two seemingly disparate themes, heaven and sex. He said we are sojourners heading home and then talked about lust, which is what sexual desire becomes when sin is added. These two have far more in common than meets the eye. I want to show you the impact one has on the other. I wrote this in *Through the Eyes of a Lion*, but don't miss it now: "To the degree that you cultivate your sense of longing for the next world, you will be able to combat the deadly hypnotizing desires of this one."[5]

Paul's tone tells us how big of a deal this is. He used the word *beg*. That's not casual. You don't resort to begging unless it is critical.

His begging is the literary equivalent of Paul Revere's midnight ride. You are under attack. The lusts are coming, the lusts are coming! They are warring against the soul. *Warring!* As in, this is war. Life is not a game to be played but a war to be waged. You have an enemy who wants to take you out because he knows what greatness lies within you. You must remember this, because you can't win a battle you don't know you're in. When you don't know Satan is there, he is capable of a surprise attack.

Peter isn't just here to warn us. He is kind enough to provide this solution: activity flows from identity.

Life is not a game to be played but a war to be waged.

What we do flows from knowing who we are. It is in knowing that we are "sojourners and pilgrims" that we have the power to "abstain from fleshly lusts." An alien is someone living away from home in a foreign country. Well, someone call Will Smith and Tommy Lee Jones, because *you* are an alien. The day you come to Christ, you become a citizen of heaven. It is your true home, even though you've never been there, and knowing that takes off the pressure to fit in.

It's easy to get bogged down in doing something you know you shouldn't because "everybody's doing it." No one wants to look weird. Newsflash: you are supposed to be strange! "For you have spent enough time in the past doing what pagans choose to do—living in debauchery, lust, drunkenness, orgies, carousing and detestable idolatry" (1 Peter 4:3 NIV), aka Coachella meets Mardi Gras. You are a stranger, a pilgrim, an alien. People from different cultures have different values and different standards. If you perfectly blend in, you're doing it wrong!

Remembering that heaven is your home also takes the

emphasis off of "living the dream" here and now. We are to focus not on our pleasure here but our treasure there. God wants you to enjoy your life here, and I believe he wants to bless you so he can bless others through you. But the goal isn't to "have it all," because you will have to leave it all. Your treasure is not in this life but in the next. You are just passing through, waiting for a city whose builder is God, a kingdom that can't be shaken. There's no stronger motivation than anticipation.

Clinging to your true destination will also change the way you view trials. If your vision is long-sighted, as it's supposed to be, your problems are mere speed bumps on the way to glory. Yes, the outward man perishes—so what? Your inward man is being renewed day by day. Next time you are tempted or tested, try this: click your heels together three times and whisper to God, "There's no place like home, and this is not it." In my most challenging moments I think of my daughter Lenya's ruby-red sparkly slippers I gave her for her final birthday on earth, and, looking beyond to my true Home, it puts my problems in perspective.

Most of all, remembering your true identity changes the way you view death. Death is not *leaving* home but *going* home. Not defeat but victory. To be absent from the body is to be present with the Lord (2 Corinthians 5:8). As Job said, "Though my skin is dissolved, with my eyes I will see God" (Job 19:26, author's paraphrase).

But the most beautiful, most freeing word in 1 Peter 2:11–12 is the first one: *beloved*.

You are loved by God. That is your identity; let your activity flow from there. Your motivation to live how God wants you to shouldn't be to earn his love, because you already have it and can never lose it.

He loves you, he loves you, he loves you. No more on your best days than on your worst day. His love isn't based on your goodness but on his own. Have a great quiet time? His love didn't go up. Look at porn again? His love didn't go down. It never wavers. His ocean of love is always full to the brim, and truly understanding this is the ultimate game changer. Stop trying to earn his approval, and start enjoying it!

YOUR CROWN IS COMING

On a bright, sunny day, Lenya and I were in Disneyland on a daddy-daughter date when all of a sudden Cinderella came up behind us and said hello. Knowing just what to do, Lenya immediately took Cinderella by the hand, and they went for a walk. Trailing behind and taking pictures, I caught only bits and pieces of the conversation, but I heard Cinderella ask Lenya if she had met Tinkerbell before. She then took Lenya around the castle, bringing us to the front of a very long line to introduce her. It was a magical moment.

I think of Lenya's homecoming like that: we were just walking along, and Jesus took her by the hand and brought her to a castle in the sky that's full of princes and princesses.

One day my time to leave for paradise will come, and so will yours. Our pilgrimages and sojourns will come to an end, and we will finally be home. On that day our suffering and sacrifices will seem small, but will be rewarded a hundredfold. All the strength that it took to rise up in honor will be eclipsed by heaven's glory and our reward.

Until that day comes, take heart.

God is whispering to you what my dentist told me after several hours of drilling at a recent appointment. He was finishing the foundation where a brand-new front tooth would be placed once it was shaped just for me in a dental lab. I was lying there with a bib around my neck and my tiny front top tooth freshly filed to a tiny stump that looked like it belonged in the mouth of Gollum. I felt as incomplete as Adam without Eve, and I was impatient, because it had just been explained to me that I wasn't going home that day with the tooth I was hoping for. The dentist sat me up, put his hand on my shoulder, looked me in the eye, and trusted me with words that exploded in my heart like circles ringing out from a skipped stone in smooth water:

"I know this has been painful and inconvenient, but it will all be worth it when your crown gets here."

MY STAND FOR STRENGTH AND HONOR

From this day forward, I choose to honor God's plan for my love life. No matter what is behind me I commit to fighting for my calling today but also for my future. If I am married, either now or in the future, I will fight to serve, love, and honor my spouse and my sons and daughters. In times of temptation I will trust God's Spirit, turn to his Word, and talk to his people. When I fall, I will get back up. God's grace is enough for me, and his strength is made perfect in my weakness. I will live with my heart set on heaven and run this race looking unto Jesus, the author and finisher of my faith. I can do nothing on my own, but all things as he gives me strength.

Signed   Date

Things I Really, Really Want You to Remember

First Samuel 17:40 tells us that David paused before the battle with Goliath; he picked up five smooth stones from a brook and put them into his shepherd's pouch. I wanted to take some of the "smoothest stones" from *Swipe Right* and make them easy to load up into your heart as you navigate your own personal battles. This section contains many of the truths we have discussed, distilled into bite-size nuggets. I hope you will get them stuck in your head and your heart intentionally so they will be there in a moment of need. The last thing you want is to be standing in front of a nine-foot-tall trial and have nothing in your pouch to fire off at it.

I have also taken all of the Scripture verses used in the book and put them all in one place. You can find this at levilusko.com/swiperightverses.

INTRODUCTION: CHAPTER ZERO

- Our goal should be progress, not perfection.
- When you take what God has told you not to touch, it

can keep you from experiencing what he wants you to have.

- Train today for the relationship you want tomorrow.
- The same forces that destroy you can propel you.
- Powerful things can be used for great good—or great damage.

CHAPTER 1: YOU DON'T WANT WHAT THE DEVIL'S GOT IN HIS CROCK-POT

- Don't trade the ultimate for the instant.
- The devil can't take you to hell, but if you let him, he will keep you from living for heaven.
- You need to know that Satan is slow cooking the death of your calling.
- If you don't understand your calling, you'll undervalue it.
- *Now* yells louder, but *later* lasts longer.

CHAPTER 2: THE PROBLEM WITH PINEAPPLES

- The devil will wait until you're run down to bring you temptation that promises relief.
- If we want God to bless our "I do," perhaps the solution is growing our "I won't" before marriage even begins.
- God has much better in store than what you would settle for.
- Sex is a treasure to be valued.

CHAPTER 3: SCARS MEAN SEX

- Porn doesn't make you better, but it will make you bitter.
- When you let sex drive, it will steer you wrong.
- Devise what you will or will not deal with down the road.

CHAPTER 4: FLYING BLIND

- Understanding God is not our job; obeying him is.
- Protect your future by living carefully right now.
- The breakthrough you are longing for might come without any indication that progress is being made.
- God doesn't want to take something from you; he has something for you.

CHAPTER 5: STRENGTH AND HONOR

- What you do with your liberty can put you back in captivity.
- It's possible to have a saved soul but a wasted life.
- You are chosen, loved, called, and equipped.
- It's not having a sex drive that is the problem; it's letting sex drive.

CHAPTER 6: THE THINGS WE CARRY

- Just as surely as we pack bags for trips, we all bring baggage with us into marriage.

- Of course God can forgive you—but he'd much rather be blessing you and using you.
- The devil wants your future to be so wracked with bad decisions and foolish choices that you can't enjoy what Jesus died for you to have.
- God specializes in redemption stories.
- Just because you can't unreap what you have already sown doesn't mean you can't start sowing something new.
- God can't even see your sin, because you are hidden in your Savior.
- What you live now, you'll lug later.

CHAPTER 7: RED BULL AT BEDTIME

- Perhaps the problem isn't what you aren't doing but what you are consuming.
- Combat your instant desires with their true cost.
- Get crazy with sin and sin will get crazy with you.

CHAPTER 8: SAMSON'S HAIR BEGAN TO GROW

- As long as your heart beats in your chest, there remains hope of a better tomorrow.
- When you fall, get back up.
- God doesn't get any pleasure out of your paying penance for things Jesus has already paid for.
- God's so good he'll bless you in places you never should have gone.

CHAPTER 9: VICE PRESIDENT BIDEN IN MY BED

- If you don't like what you're attracting, do something to attract something else.
- Marrying the wrong person isn't even the biggest problem; being the wrong person is.
- Don't focus on playing the field, but reaching the world.

CHAPTER 10: DATE YOUR MATE—OR THE DEVIL WILL FIND SOMEONE WHO WILL

- Jesus will come into any situation where he is invited.
- God puts to use what we offer him.
- If you don't date your mate, the devil will find someone who will.
- You'll never be right with your mate until you're right with your maker.

CHAPTER 11: BREAKING THE FOURTH WALL

- The most painful thing you have endured is the very thing God wants to use to unleash power in your life.
- You have never, for even one second, been apart from God.
- God wants to reward your victories, not rub your nose in your history.

- God's presence is not based on your performance.
- You have the choice to dwell on hardship or rejoice that God drew you out.

CONCLUSION: WINTER IS COMING

- Victory comes to those who can see past the seed.
- Let God prepare you and believe that he is also preparing someone for you.
- Live below with your heart set on his kingdom above.

A GIFT FOR YOU
SWIPE RIGHT STICKER PACK
✦ ✦ ✦

For those times when you need little reminders to train today for the relationship you want tomorrow.

Strategically put these stickers in places where you can see them in times of temptation or in moments of discouragement.

Request your *free* sticker pack at
www.levilusko.com/SwipeRightGift

Acknowledgments

When I sat down to write *Swipe Right* on December 31, 2015, my mind played tricks on me. Following up a book so personal and special as *Through the Eyes of a Lion* was intimidating. So instead of trying to recapture lightning in a bottle, I made it my explicit goal to write to help people. I invited different individuals into the chair in my mind as I wrote: some young, innocent, and blissfully naive, and others who were worn down by life and bad decisions. It was not my goal to write a great book but instead to move my reader's life forward. Whether this book is critically acclaimed or completely unknown, if you are reading this it means you have stuck with me to the end, and I pray that it has helped *you*. From my heart, thank you for going with me on this journey.

Jennie, thank you for endless encouragement, friendship, and love. You, Alivia, Daisy, and Clover are beauty, fun, laughter, encouragement, escape, and madness just when I need it. Lenya, from heaven you inspire me as I run this race. We are moving closer to you and not further away. I miss you.

Dad, thank you for being an example of a godly man to me every day of my life. Mom, your compassion and empathy are a beautiful thing. I want to be more like you.

To the whole team at Fresh Life, and in particular those close to the *Swipe Right* fire (Chelsea, Amanda, HJ, Elisha, John Mark, and Kevin), thank you for your dedication and passion. You are the lion. Thank you, Josh Noom, for a BA cover. To the crew at W: I have thoroughly enjoyed being on this journey with you and am consistently blessed by your heart to reach people. Lori and Kristi, your hearts consistently shine. Debbie, your love for Jesus and belief in me is relentlessly encouraging. Meaghan, you are an amazing editor, and I am grateful for you. The process is a struggle, but you made this a better book. Mr. Robinson and Mr. Johnson thank you, as do all my many chemically imbalanced personalities. To my literary agent, Austin, this is it, buddy. I am never writing again! But let's talk soon—I'm sure the next one will be awesome.

I want to thank Pastor Andy Stanley for two things: for preaching the message on Appetites at Passion 2011, which forever changed how I looked at the soup served from Jacob to Esau, and for a teaching series that has been published and preached under a few different names. I first heard it under the heading "The New Rules for Love, Sex, and Dating." Those talks are some of the best relationship messages I have ever heard, and I am indebted to him for many thoughts and ideas because of seeds sown while listening to this content. Pastor Louie Giglio's series "Boy Meets Girl" also had a very powerful influence on the way I view and communicate about relationships as a form of and outflow of worship.

Pastor Greg Laurie was with me in the snow during Femur-Mageddeon, and in life in general he has had my back.

My brother Jesse sent me a *Vanity Fair* article about

Acknowledgments

Tinder, and it was while reading the article that I was struck with the idea for calling my yet unnamed relationship book *Swipe Right*. Thank you, Jesse. To Lysa TerKeurst I am indebted for many things. It was she who helped me nail down the right subtitle for the book; helped our team become more compelling communicators; gave me the idea for the "Things I Really, Really Want You to Remember" section at the back of the book; and encouraged and affirmed me as a writer. I'm still trying to take those negative thoughts captive. Lysa, thank you!

Jennie and I have been communicating the content that is contained in these pages ever since we were gripped with a calling to do so while on our honeymoon in Maui in 2004.

To see the twelve years of these O2 Experience events culminate in the book you are holding is overwhelmingly beautiful. I have lost my voice countless times preaching about being a snakebird and about the devil's Crock-Pot and about getting back up, but now it is safely committed to the ages—ink on a page is immune to laryngitis. I am grateful that Jesus trusted me with this message and pray that the reach continues to ring out to infinity and beyond.

Notes

INTRODUCTION: CHAPTER ZERO

1. Stephen Willard, "Study: People Check Their Cell Phones Every Six Minutes, 150 Times a Day," *Elite Daily*, February 11, 2013, http://elitedaily.com/news/world/study-people -check\-cell-phones-minutes-150-times-day/.
2. David Pierce, "The Oral History of Tinder's Alluring Right Swipe," *Wired*, September 28, 2016, https://www.wired.com /2016/09/history-of-tinder-right-swipe/.
3. Nancy Jo Sales, "Tinder and the Dawn of the 'Dating Apocalypse,'" *Vanity Fair*, August 6, 2015, http://www .vanityfair.com/culture/2015/08/tinder-hook-up-culture-end -of-dating.
4. Ibid.
5. Ibid.
6. Alex Morris, "Tales from the Millennials' Sexual Revolution," *Rolling Stone*, March 31, 2014, http://www.rollingstone.com /feature/millennial-sexual-revolution-relationships-marriage #ixzz2yv15mrS8.
7. Justin R. Garcia, Sean G. Massey, Ann M. Merriwether, Susan M. Seibold-Simpson, "Orgasm Experience Among Emerging Adult Men and Women: Relationship Context and Attitudes Toward Uncommitted Sex," poster presented at the 25th Association for Psychological Science Convention, Washington, DC, May 26, 2013,

https://aps.psychologicalscience.org/convention/program_
2013/search/viewProgram.cfm?Abstract_ID=28800&Ab
Type=&AbAuthor=253854&Subject_ID=&Day_ID=all&
keyword=.

8. Brenda Major, et al., "Report of the Task Force on Mental
Health and Abortion" (Washington, DC: American
Psychological Association, 2008), http://www.apa.org/pi
/wpo/mental-health-abortion-report.pdf.

9. Mark Banschick, "The High Failure Rate of Second and
Third Marriages: Why Are Second and Third Marriages
More Likely to Fail?" *The Intelligent Divorce* (blog),
Psychology Today, February 6, 2012, https://www
.psychologytoday.com/blog/the-intelligent-divorce/201202
/the-high-failure-rate-second-and-third-marriages.

10. C. S. Lewis, *Surprised by Joy: The Shape of My Early Life*
(Orlando: Harcourt, 1955), 226.

CHAPTER 1: YOU DON'T WANT WHAT THE DEVIL'S GOT IN HIS CROCK-POT

1. Jentezen Franklin's Facebook page, accessed October 4,
2016, https://www.facebook.com/JentezenFranklin
/posts/681872325209209.

2. Andy Stanley, "Andy Stanley—A Bowl of Stew . . . ,"
YouTube video, 42:10, from an address at the Passion
Conference in Atlanta, GA, on January 3, 2011, posted by
"All Passion Sermons," September 26, 2016, https://www
.youtube.com/watch?v=6DcSjabCY1l.

3. Phil Knight, *Shoe Dog: A Memoir by the Creator of Nike*,
Kindle ed. (New York: Scribner, 2016), loc. 5403–5.

CHAPTER 2: THE PROBLEM WITH PINEAPPLES

1. "Why We Hate Cheap Things," *The Book of Life* (blog),
http://www.thebookoflife.org/why-we-hate-cheap-things/.

2. Suzanne Raga, "The Super Luxe History of Pineapples (and Why They Used to Cost $8000)," *Mental Floss*, June 25, 2015, http://mentalfloss.com/article/65506/super-luxe -history-pineapples-and-why-they-used-cost-8000.

3. "Why We Hate Cheap Things."

4. Ibid.

CHAPTER 3: SCARS MEAN SEX

1. *Island of the Mega Shark*, aired July 12, 2015 on the Discovery Channel, transcript available at http://tv.ark .com/transcript/island_of_the_mega_shark/61/DSCP /Sunday_July_12_2015/845978/.

2. Meg Meeker, *Strong Fathers, Strong Daughters: 10 Secrets Every Father Should Know* (New York: Ballantine, 2007), 19.

3. Nick Anderson and Scott Clement, "1 in 5 College Women Say They Were Violated," *Washington Post*, June 12, 2015, http://www.washingtonpost.com/sf/local/2015/06/12/1-in-5 -women-say-they-were-violated/?tid=a_inl.

4. National Sexual Violence Resource Center, "Statistics About Sexual Violence," 2015, http://www.nsvrc.org/sites /default/files/publications_nsvrc_factsheet_media-packet _statistics-about-sexual-violence_0.pdf.

5. I first heard this argument raised in Andy Stanley's preaching series, *The New Rules for Love, Sex and Dating*, April–May 2011, http://northpoint.org/messages/the-new -rules-for-love-sex-and-dating.

6. Louie Giglio, *Boy Meets Girl* (Atlanta: Passion City Church Resources, 2012), DVD.

CHAPTER 4: FLYING BLIND

1. Ed Vulliamy, "Why Kennedy Crashed," *Guardian*, July 25, 1999, https://www.theguardian.com/world/1999/jul/25 /kennedy.usa.

2. C. S. Lewis, *Mere Christianity* (New York: MacMillan, 1958), 104.

CHAPTER 5: STRENGTH AND HONOR

1. Allan Brettman, "Creator of Nike's Famed Swoosh Remembers Its Conception 40 Years Later," *Oregonian*, June 15, 2011, http://www.oregonlive.com/business/index .ssf/2011/06/nikes_swoosh_brand_logo_hits_4.html.

2. Horace Mann, quoted in Noble G. Rice, "That Boy," *Western Journal of Education* 2, no. 5 (October 1896): 3.

3. C. S. Lewis, "Learning in War-Time," *The Weight of Glory: and Other Addresses* (1949; repr. New York: HarperOne, 2001), 47.

4. Bill Hendrick, "Benefits in Delaying Sex Until Marriage," WebMD, December 28, 2010, http://www.webmd.com/sex -relationships/news/20101227/theres-benefits-in-delaying -sex-until-marriage.

5. Robert E. Rector, Kirk A. Johnson, Lauren R. Noyes, Shannan Martin, "The Harmful Effects of Early Sexual Activity and Multiple Sexual Partners Among Women: A Book of Charts," (Washington, DC: Heritage Foundation, 2003), https://thf_media.s3.amazonaws.com/2003/pdf /Bookofcharts.pdf.

6. Jud Wilhite, *That Crazy Little Thing Called Love: The Soundtrack of Marriage, Sex, and Faith* (Cincinnati: Standard, 2007), 75.

7. Belinda Luscombe, "How to Stay Married," *Time*, June 13, 2016, 40.

8. Note to parents: This is a great illustration to teach young children to honor themselves. You can bring these three different cups out, one at a time, and talk about how you treat the cups differently depending on their value. It's a sticky visual to convey that your children have intrinsic worth and should live accordingly.

9. Biz Stone, "Timing Lessons," *Biz Stone*, September 3, 2010, http://www.bizstone.com/2010/09/timing-lessons.html.

10. David W. Wiersbe and Warren W. Wiersbe, *C Is for Christmas: The History, Personalities, and Meaning of Christ's Birth* (Grand Rapids: Baker, 2012), 179.

CHAPTER 6: THE THINGS WE CARRY

1. Andy Stanley, *The New Rules for Love, Sex and Dating*, April–May 2011, http://northpoint.org/messages/the-new-rules-for-love-sex-and-dating.

2. "Get Informed About Human Trafficking," Department of Children and Families (CT), accessed October 6, 2016, http://www.ct.gov/dcf/cwp/view.asp?a=4127&Q=492900.

3. "Child Welfare and Human Trafficking," Child Welfare Information Gateway, July 2015, https://www.childwelfare.gov/pubPDFs/trafficking.pdf.

4. Susan Kay Hunter and K.C. Reed, "Taking the Side of Bought and Sold Rape," speech at National Coalition Against Sexual Assault, Washington, DC, 1990, quoted in Melissa Farley and Emily Butler, "Prostitution and Trafficking—Quick Facts," Prostitution Research and Education, 2012, http://www.prostitutionresearch.com/Prostitution%20Quick%20Facts%2012-21-12.pdf.

5. Chris Blake, "Nearly 46 Million People Trapped in Modern-Day Slavery, Report Finds," *Bloomberg*, May 30, 2016, http://www.bloomberg.com/news/articles/2016-05-31/nearly-46-million-people-trapped-in-modern-slavery-report-finds.

6. Jim Kavanagh, "Abolishing Sex Slavery by Helping One Girl at a Time," CNN, June 16, 2011, http://thecnnfreedomproject.blogs.cnn.com/2011/06/16/abolishing-sex-slavery-by-helping-one-girl-at-a-time/.

7. Melissa Farley et al, "Prostitution and Trafficking in Nine Countries: An Update on Violence and Post-Traumatic

Stress Disorder," in Melissa Farley, ed., *Prostitution, Trafficking, and Traumatic Stress* (Binghamton, NY: Routledge, 2003), 48.

8. *Wikipedia*, s.v. "Hope chest," last modified July 19, 2016, https://en.wikipedia.org/wiki/Hope_chest.

CHAPTER 7: RED BULL AT BEDTIME

1. Mindy Kaling, "Branch Wars," *The Office*, season 4, episode 10, directed by Joss Whedon, aired November 1, 2007 (Universal City, CA: Universal Home Entertainment, 2014), DVD.

2. Philip G. Zimbardo and Nikita Duncan, "'The Demise of Guys': How Video Games and Porn Are Ruining a Generation," *CNN*, May 24, 2012, http://edition.cnn.com/2012/05/23/health/living-well/demise-of-guys/index.html.

3. Ibid.

4. Russell Brand, interview with Conan O'Brien, *Conan*, TBS, November 8, 2012, http://teamcoco.com/video/russell-brands-olympic-sex-ventures.

5. Russell Brand, interview with Piers Morgan, "Men of the Year: 2006, Russell Brand," *British GQ*, October 2006, http://www.gq-magazine.co.uk/article/russell-brand-interview-piers-morgan-most-stylish-fashion-2006.

6. Russell Brand, "50 Shades—Has Porn Ruined My Chance of a Happy Marriage? Russell Brand The Trews (E261)," YouTube video, February 20, 2015, https://www.youtube.com/watch?v=R6GdEnINhtQ.

7. Alex Dickinson, "Helping Kids With Habits Elders Never Had," July 23, 2012, http://www.strugglingteens.com/artman/publish/printer_MountPleasantBN_120913.shtml.

8. Belinda Luscombe, "Porn and the Threat to Virility," *Time*, April 11, 2016, 42.

9. "Romance Industry Statistics," Romance Writers of

America, accessed October 13, 2016, https://www.rwa.org
/p/cm/ld/fid=580.

10. "Erotica Boom Affects Genre Book Sales," BBC, August 22,
2012, http://www.bbc.com/news/entertainment-arts
-19341735.

11. Norman Doidge, "Brain Scans of Porn Addicts: What's
Wrong with This Picture?" *Guardian* (UK), September 26,
2013, https://www.theguardian.com/commentisfree/2013
/sep/26/brain-scans-porn-addicts-sexual-tastes.

12. "How to Outrun a Cheetah," a clip from "Savannah,"
Speed Kills, season 1, episode 1, aired October 7, 2012
(Washington, DC: Smithsonian Channel, 2012), http://
www.smithsonianchannel.com/videos/how-to-outrun-a
-cheetah/18332.

CHAPTER 8: SAMSON'S HAIR BEGAN TO GROW

1. Leland Ryken, James C. Wilhoit, Tremper Longman III,
eds., *Dictionary of Biblical Imagery* (Downers Grove, IL:
IVP Academic, 1998), s.v. "seven."

2. *Rocky Balboa*, directed by Sylvester Stallone (2006; Sony
Pictures Home Entertainment, 2007), DVD.

3. Jon Ronson, "How One Stupid Tweet Blew Up Justine
Sacco's Life," *New York Times Magazine*, February 12,
2015, http://www.nytimes.com/2015/02/15/magazine/how
-one-stupid-tweet-ruined-justine-saccos-life.html?_r=0.

4. Ibid.

5. Neal Colgrass, "Ex-CFO Who Slammed Chick-fil-A Lives
on Food Stamps," *Newser*, March 28, 2015; repr. *USA
Today*, March 29, 2015, http://www.usatoday.com/story
/money/2015/03/29/adam-smith-chick-fil-a-video-memoir
/70629290/.

6. "Reporting Sexual Assault: Why Survivors Often Don't,"

Maryland Coalition Against Sexual Assault (Silver Spring, MD: n.d.), accessed October 13, 2016, http://www.umd .edu/ocrsm/files/Why-Is-Sexual-Assault-Under-Reported.pdf.

CHAPTER 9: VICE PRESIDENT BIDEN IN MY BED

1. "Jack's Smirking Revenge," *Fight Club*, directed by David Fincher (1999; Los Angeles: 20th Century Fox, 2002), DVD.
2. Tommy Nelson, "Solomon on Romance (Part 1 of 2)," sermon, *Focus on the Family Daily Broadcast*, February 24, 2015, radio broadcast, http://www.focusonthefamily.com /media/daily-broadcast/solomon-on-romance-pt1.
3. Andy Stanley, *The New Rules for Love, Sex, and Dating* (Grand Rapids: Zondervan, 2014), 50.
4. Craig Groeschel, *From This Day Forward: Five Commitments to Fail-Proof Your Marriage* (Grand Rapids: Zondervan, 2014), 28.
5. Meg Meeker, *Strong Fathers, Strong Daughters: 10 Secrets Every Father Should Know* (New York: Ballantine, 2007), 100.
6. Steven Reinberg, "One in Four Girls Have STDs," *U.S. News and World Report*, November 23, 2009, http://health .usnews.com/health-news/family-health/cancer/articles/2009 /11/23/one-in-four-teen-girls-have-stds.
7. Meeker, *Strong Fathers*, 106.
8. C. S. Lewis, *Mere Christianity* (1952; repr. New York: HarperOne, 2001), 105.

CHAPTER 10: DATE YOUR MATE—OR THE DEVIL WILL FIND SOMEONE WHO WILL

1. "Spielberg: A Director's Life Reflected in Film," *60 Minutes*, October 21, 2012, interviewed by Lesley Stahl.
2. Cal Fussman, "Dr. Dre: What I've Learned," *Esquire*,

December 11, 2013, http://www.esquire.com/entertainment /music/news/a23843/dr-dre-interview-0114/.

CHAPTER 11: BREAKING THE FOURTH WALL

1. "Induced Abortion in the United States," Guttmacher Institute, September 2016, https://www.guttmacher.org/fact -sheet/induced-abortion-united-states.

2. Philip Henry, *Notes of Conversations with the Duke of Wellington, 1831–1851* (London: John Murray, 1888), 9.

3. Robert Morris, *The God I Never Knew: How Real Friendship with the Holy Spirit Can Change Your Life* (Colorado Springs: Waterbrook, 2011), 47.

4. A. W. Tozer, *The Pursuit of God*, updated ed. (Abbotsford, WI: Aneko Press, 2015), 50.

5. Oliver Holden, "Secret Prayer," *The Young Convert's Companion, Being a Collection of Hymns for the Use of Conference Meetings* (Boston: E. Lincoln, 1806); repr. in Charles S. Sutter and Wilbur F. Tillett, *The Hymns and Hymn Writers of the Church: An Annotated Edition of the Methodist Hymnal* (New York: Eaton & Mains, 1911), 272.

6. Bob Simon, "The Recyclers: From Trash Comes Triumph," *60 Minutes*, November 17, 2013, http://www.cbsnews.com /news/recyclers-from-trash-comes-triumph-2/; Regina Wang, "The Recycled Orchestra: Slum Children Create Music out of Garbage," *Time*, December 11, 2012, http://newsfeed .time.com/2012/12/11/watch-the-recycled-orchestra-slum -children-create-music-out-of-garbage/.

CONCLUSION: WINTER IS COMING

1. Mike Berardino, "Mike Tyson Explains One of His Most Famous Quotes," *Sun Sentinel*, November 9, 2012, http:// articles.sun-sentinel.com/2012-11-09/sports/sfl-mike-tyson

-explains-one-of-his-most-famous-quotes-20121109_1_mike -tyson-undisputed-truth-famous-quotes.

2. Robert Schuller, *Life Changers* (New York: F. H. Revell, 1981), 141.

3. William Shakespeare, *Richard III*, 1.1.1–2.

4. "Single Serving Jack," *Fight Club*, directed by David Fincher (1999; Los Angeles: 20th Century Fox, 2002), DVD.

5. Levi Lusko, *Through the Eyes of a Lion: Facing Impossible Pain, Finding Incredible Power* (Nashville: W Publishing, 2015), 137.

About the Author

Abby Sue Carlson

Levi Lusko is a bestselling author, pastor of Fresh Life Church (a multisite church in Montana and Utah), and the founder of Skull Church and the O2 Experience. Levi travels around the world speaking about Jesus. He takes pleasure in small things, such as black coffee, new shoes, and fast Internet, and falling asleep in the sun. He and his wife, Jennie, have four daughters: Alivia, Daisy, Clover, and Lenya, who is in heaven.

ALSO AVAILABLE FROM LEVI LUSKO

★ ★ ★

This can't be real.

These thoughts swim through my mind and try to strangle me. My heart is shattered into a thousand pieces, each shard jagged and razor sharp. The pain is surreal, deafening, and catastrophic. My eyes burn. I want to cry, but the tears won't come. I want to scream, but it won't help. I am afraid. But I'm not alone....

You must not rely on the naked eye. What you think you see is not all that is there. There are unseen things. Spiritual things. Eternal things. You must learn to see life through the eyes of a Lion. Doing so is to utilize the telescope of faith, which will not only allow you to perceive the invisible—it will give you the strength to do the impossible.

From the introduction of Levi Lusko's book,
Through the Eyes of a Lion.

Through the Eyes of a Lion will help you:

Embrace the power of hope in a world that is often filled with suffering and loss.

Discover a manifesto for high-octane living when grief and despair are paralyzing.

Learn how to let your pain become your platform.

• • •

LeviLusko.com
Available wherever books and ebooks are sold.

Church and small group resources also available!